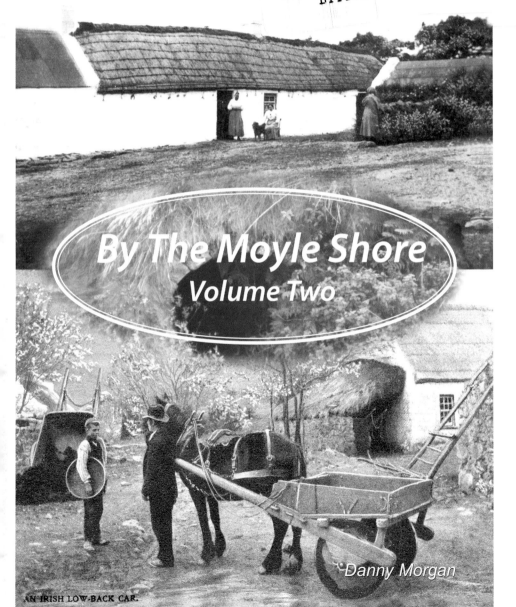

McNeills Cottage, Fair Head.

D1111353

By The Moyle Shore
Volume Two

Danny Morgan

AN IRISH LOW-BACK CAR.

©   Dalriada Publishing 2006
35 Mayo Drive
Ballycastle
Co. Antrim
BT54 6EH
028 207 69608

Front Cover: McNeills Cottage, Fair Head (top)
*   Browns Farm, Broughmore, Glenshesk*
*   North Star Mine (centre)*

This book is dedicated to Alex and May Morgan.

Acknowledgements

Glens of Antrim Historical Society for permission to quote from a number of their publications.

Fiachra Mac Gabhann, Partry, Co. Mayo, for permission to quote from "Place-names of Northern Ireland," Volume Seven, published by The Institute of Irish Studies, The Queens University of Belfast, 1997.

Edward J Bourke Dublin, for permission to quote from "Shipwrecks of the Irish Coast" (two volumes).

G.D.Downing-Fullerton and Hugh Clarke for permission to quote from records of the Ballycastle Estate, held by Greer Hamilton & Gailey, Ballymoney.

Ann Marie McClarey, formerly with Moyle One Stop Shop, Ballycastle, for her advice and assistance.

Heather Apsley formerly with the Ballycastle Community Development Office.

Frank Rodgers, Ballycastle for producing maps of the Craigfad coalmine.

Nick Moffet, Ballycastle Community Development Office, for his advice and assistance.

The staff of NEELB Library at Ballycastle, Ballymoney, Ballymena and Coleraine.

Eileen Christie, Ballycastle, Anne, Sinead and Orla Kelly, Ballycastle for compiling the data.

Mary and Emma Chambers, Portballintrae for preparatory work on the book.

Andrew, Danny and Jayne McGill, Ballinlea, for proof reading.

Peter Molloy, Ballycastle, for the loan of maps.

Ciaran Morgan, for his assistance in the preparatory work.

Joe Butler, Ballyvoy, for his information which came in too late for inclusion in this volume.

Hugh McGill, for his photography work.

Jimmy McVeigh, Acravally, for photographs.

The sponsors of the book, whose assistance is greatly appreciated, as the book has been produced without any grant aid. Moyle District Council was approached seeking a small grant towards publication. I never even received a reply.

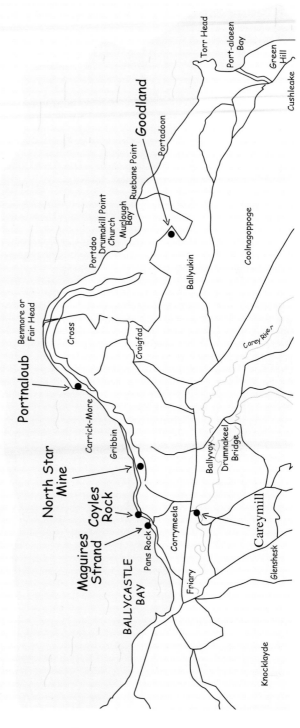

Portnaloub

Goodland

Benmore or
Fair Head

North Star
Mine

Coyles
Rock

Maguires
Strand

BALLYCASTLE
BAY

Careymill

Torr Head

Port-alaeen
Bay

Green
Hill

Cushleake

Portadoon

Ruebane Point

Mullough
Bay

Drumakill Point
Church

Portdoo

Coolnagoppoge

Ballyukin

Cross

Craigfad

Carey River

Carrick-More

Gribbin

Ballyvoy

Drumnakeel
Bridge

Corrymeela

Pans Rock

Friary

Glenshesk

Knocklayde

7

Introduction

Volume Two of 'By The Moyle Shore' follows on from where Volume One left off, but this time the focus is on Culfeightrin Parish. The stretch of land from the Margy River to Torr is examined and this is followed by an exploration of the Fair Head area.

Coal and iron ore mines, saltworks, scythe-stone production and quarrying were at one time important industries in Carey. Some of the old trades and families featured include Clarke, Coyle, Darragh, Dillon, Duffin, Laverty, McBride, McCormick, McKinley, McMichael, Meehan and O'Mullan.

The enigmatic sculptured face at the Pans Rocks, the death of Fr. James McCann and the story of Julia McQuillan (Black nun) are covered here.

Much material relating to Carey has been omitted and must await another publication, the planned triology expanding to a fourth volume.

Danny Morgan
October, 2006

Chapter One -

The Margy To The North Star Dyke

The ancient territory of Carey has for a short stretch of its boundary the river immortalised by John Henry Macauley's famous song " The Oul Lammas Fair".

The "silver Margy" divides Ballycastle and the Parish of Ramoan from its neighbour, Culfeightrin. Better known today as Carey which is an early tribal name, comparable with Kerry and Offaly.[1]

Robert A. Wilson who was born at Dunfanaghy, Co. Donegal c 1820, was a journalist and poet who commemorated the Margy in the poem, "River, River, Rippling River".

His mother Catherine was the daughter of Alex Hunter of Dunnamallaght, Ballycastle, and his father Arthur Wilson had been a coastguard here. After some years Catherine returned to live in her father's house, later she moved with her two sons and two daughters to a cottage in the Maguires Strand area.

This was the childhood background of the native Gaelic speaker who wrote under the pen-name Barney Maglone. He died in Belfast, 10th August 1875 and was buried in the City Cemetery.[2]

At Drumahammond Bridge the Carey River and Glenshesk River unite to form the Margy River. The adjacent townland of Bonamargy signifies the end or bottom of the Margy.

This has traditionally been translated as meaning market, but boundary has recently been suggested.[3]

Julia McQuillan was a pious hermit who flourished in the 17th century. She resided in Bonamargy and is remembered for a number of prophecies.
One was that foreign soldiers with snow on their helmets would land at Ballycastle and afterwards the Margy would run red with blood.[4]

During severe winters the river froze over, locals skated on the ice, and one man cycled between the footbridge and the Margy's Bridge. Circuses once came regularly to what is now the Golf Links. Near the Cushendall Road entrance the big top was erected at a spot known as the Circus Ring. The name was recorded in an 1890 Chronicle, but is now obsolete.[6] When the Gaelic Athletic Association was established in Ballycastle in 1907, the new club used a field which lay between the friary ruins and the Carey River.

This location no doubt influenced the club's name, the McQuillans, as they were credited as having established Bonamargy Friary in the late 15th century (the McCormicks and the McDonnells also claimed the honour). Hurling was also played in Jack Thompson's field, off Bleachgreen Avenue before moving to Leyland Road.

Playing hurling on the strand, especially at Christmas, has a long tradition in Co.Antrim, and elsewhere.
Although there is no evidence for this at Ballycastle, it would be surprising if the game was not played here in bygone centuries.[7]

Ballycastle Golf Club was formed in 1890, and shortly afterwards a 9 hole course was laid out on The Warren. Earlier in 1882 a sports track was constructed over looking the Strand, and here the Annual Sports were held for many years. [8]

One Ballycastle man recalled as a boy rolling his Easter eggs along the road at The Warren, there was very little traffic then. [9]

Tramway
At certain periods of the year, usually in late Summer or early Autumn one may observe 2 rows of stakes curving across the Margy.

River Margy showing pilework and tramway site

They are the remains of Hugh Boyd's pile-work when he changed the course of the river during the construction of Ballycastle Harbour, 1738-1743.

A row of 3 oak piles jut out at an angle from the East bank. Beyond them are two more, and further out are another pair. They are the remains of a wooden bridge which carried Boyd's tramway to the collieries. A few years ago during dredging operations timbers from near the bridge site, were thrown up on the river bank.

Pile, showing its tapered point with the imprints of iron straps

One was approximately eleven feet long, while the other was a broken stump with a neatly tapered point which had been shod with iron. This was clearly shown by the imprints of an iron strap on each of the 4 sides.

The tramway having crossed the river swung left, then ran in a straight line across the sand dunes to Bath Lodge, and on towards Carrickmore.[10]

Sand from the Strand supplied the needs of local farmers who paid per cart load. The late Hugh A. Boyd recalled farmers approaching from the Marine Hotel direction. With their horses and carts they forded the Margy, then followed the lane up around Glenshesk House.

When the Golf Club erected railings around their premises and had steps constructed where previously there had been none, this effectively rerouted the carters.

Ballycastle Strand showing carters c1900

Before the establishment of the links, the area had been rough ground with an abundance of whins. There was a right of way known as the Miners Path which ran at an angle from the Cushendall Road over to the edge of the Strand.

Postcards of the 1920's-30's period show a number of bathing boxes on the Strand. This was a Council owned facility, bathers paid 2 pence to undress and dress in privacy. They also had the security of knowing that their personal belongings and valuables were safely locked away.

A caretaker collected the fees and generally maintained the bathing boxes. Bella McGuile worked here in1938, accompanied on occasions by her grandson Mickie who recalled carrying buckets of water up to the boxes, in order that the visitors could wash the sand of their feet. For this service the bow received a tip.[12]

The Mendip Range

This vessel was beached on Ballycastle Strand, as a result of hostilities on 17th October 1917.[13] The incident occured about 100 yards from the start of the Strand, and was witnessed by Dickie Duffin, then a young boy. He recalled seeing tins of condensed milk, bags of flour and also containers of paraffin and petrol, bobbing up and down in the surf. Locals salvaged what they could before the authorities clamped down on such activity. By then Dickie had managed to rescue some flour, which his mother soon put to good use.

Two or three locals jointly composed a poem on the Mendip Range but their efforts were mediocre and the ballad was quickly forgotten.[14]

Flour from the vessel was sold off at public auction- a bag was purchased by the Clarkes of Ann Street. Although the outer skin had caked hard, the flour inside this layer was fine for baking with.[15]

Bath Lodge

The section of the Carrickmore Road from The Warren to the first corner was constructed in the 1790's. During the work a cist grave was discovered containing human remains, 2 querns, 2 bronze hatchets and a sword. [16]

Boyd's tramway to the mines had by then been abandoned and the track from this point eastwards became the road which we see today.

A fort known simply as Doon overlooks the 2 black rocks on the strand. Another fort called Dunrainey is located beyond Bonamargy Friary, both are located within the perimeter of Ballycastle Golf course.

Bath Lodge is an old farmhouse which pre-dates the Boyd period of mining. The date 1874 on a roadside gable commemorates the construction of an upper storey. Bath Lodge was once reached by a lane which ran from the Cushendall Road down to a bungalow named "Kilcraig". The lane then proceeded down the present drive-way to the Carrickmore Road.[17]

Prior to the invention of Morse code, Lloyds of London kept specially trained pigeons at the rear of a house at Bath Lodge. The pigeon-house has long since been demolished.[18]

Doon, Bonamargy townland with Rathlin in the background

Pans Rocks

The outcrop of rock at the end of the strand is The Pans Rock, often referred to simply as the Pans. In a pool across the footbridge, poor people once went for a seaweed bath. The practice gave this corner the name Bath Rock, now long obsolete.

When a house was built nearby it was named Bath Lodge and when a mine was opened on the opposite of the road it was called the Bath Lodge Pit.[19]

The point of The Pans was known as The Gib and off-shore in line with the Back Avenue is the Scarf Rock.[20]

This was one of a number of locations where the cormorant (Gaelic scarbh) dried out, and rested after fishing.

Carved face at the Pans Rocks, photograph by Hugh McGill

Another off-shore rock is more mysterious with a life sized human face staring out across the water. Eighty years ago it was widely believed that the sculpture had been done by some artist in memory of his wife who had drowned here. The story has no foundation as the work was executed by Charles Darragh about the year 1890 when he worked on stone for Ballycastle chapel.[21]

There is a second face at the side of steps cut at the end of a concreted path. This is a cruder carving and is said to have been done by Andy Verdon when he was an apprentice stonemason.[22]

The Verdons

The family arrived in Ballycastle in the 1860's, Andrew is listed as a leathercutter here by 1870.[23] At the same time A.Verdon is given as a spirit dealer, and this may in fact be the same person.

Andrew died 2/3/1875 aged 40, his wife Jane died 17/5/1916 aged 81. Their son Andrew, stonemason, died 3/2/1905 aged 40. A daughter Fanny Sinclair died 29/10/1927, and her sister Mary Jane McKeague died 16/2/1928 aged 58.
The Verdons had licensed premises in Castle Street and North Street, the latter is presently the Harbour Bar. When the family died with out issue, both pubs passed to their McKeague relations who have retained ownership to the present day.[24]

Andy Verdon, Junior, lived in the bar at the Quay and he was a regular swimmer at the Pans Rocks. He is said to have carved the second face over a number of Sunday afternoons. Verdon worked with Charles Darragh on a number of projects including the O'Connor Monument in the Diamond (1899).[25]

It would appear that after Darragh carved the first face, Verdon then decided to emulate the master craftsman by executing a similar work.

But the mystery is why McCahan mentions only the work done by Darragh, when he must have been aware of Verdon's carving?

Darragh Family
Charles was the stonemason who worked and dressed the first stone of St.Patrick and St.Bridid's Church, Ballycastle on 7th June 1870. The parish records state that he also worked and dressed the last stone of the chapel spire on 17th July 1890. He lived with his sister Rose at 14 North Street (now Boyles shop), a few doors from Verdon's pub.[26]

The Darraghs are an old Carey family who have been associated with the Fair Head area from at least 1669 when a Dunkan Darroch was recorded at Ballyreagh.[27] The late Andy McKinley believed that the Darraghs originated on Colonsay, an island to the north of Islay. There are in the graveyard of Bonamargy two 18th century headstones to the family. One is inscribed;

HERE
LYETH YE BODY
OF JOHN DARAGH
WHO DIED APRIL
YE 1st 1741 AGED
62 YEARS

The second stone now barely legible was recorded by Francis Joseph Bigger over a century ago.[28]

HERE LYETH THE BODY
OF JOHN DARAGH WHO DIED
AUGUST Y 15th 1745 AGED 1
YEAR ALSO ESTHER DAR
AGH DIED MAY YE 22nd 1744
AGED 2 YEARS CHILDREN
TO ARCHBALD DARAGH
ALSO THE SD ARCHBALD
DIED APRIL THE 11th
1762 AGED 45 YEARS

Dan the most prominent member of the family was born about 1836 at Lisnacalliagh in Ballyreagh Upper. Here his parents farmed a few acres, but during the Famine they were evicted from their home out on to the snow covered ground. They were given shelter by neighbours called McGrath, who were said to have also been relations of the Darraghs.

This experience had a profound effect upon Dan who became a teacher. He taught at Cushendun from 1856-8, then 2 years at Glenshesk before he became Principal of the old National School in Fairhill Street, Ballycastle.

As an active member of the Irish Republican Brotherhood, his activities came to the notice of the school authorities. When they sacked him Dan promptly established his own school at Cool Brae, in Glenshesk. Then, forced to go the run went to Scotland where he spent 6 weeks recruiting amongst the Irish emigrants of Clydebank and Coatbridge.

In 1867 Darragh was active in Birmingham, Manchester and Wolverhampton, where he was caught in the possession of arms. Convicted in April,1869 he was sentenced to a long term of imprisonment in Millbank Prison. Here he suffered harsh treatment, and in failing health he died in June 1870.

Dan Darragh (1836 – 1870)

Ballyveely School, Glenshesk

His remains were brought back to Ballycastle, where they were interred in St. Patrick and St. Brigid's new cemetery.[29] This is the man who is commemorated by the Dan Darragh Flute Band, Ballycastle. Two emigrants who booked their passage through Sharpe & McKinley's agency were John and Patrick Darragh. The former was a 24 year old carpenter who emigrated 16/4/1870 to New York. The other man who emigrated to New York in November, 1874 is unusual in that he was aged 75. Their home address was not recorded.

Ballymena born John McKenzie taught at Fairhill Street in the late 1860's. He was an accomplished musician who composed a number of tunes including "The Pans Rocks Waltz" and the "Craignascarf Polka".[30] The latter place name is now obsolete, and the Cormorants Rock lies buried somewhere underneath the new breakwater at Ballycastle. Another piece of music which may be associated with the area is the "Lament of Deirdre for the Children of Uisnech" which was collected by Edward Bunting. "Time immemorial this rock has been known as Carrig-Uisnech" writes Hill in 1873. Centuries of tradition relate that Deirdre and the sons of Uisneach landed at the Pans Rock, on their return from Loch Etive in Scotland. The story ends with the death of the three brothers by treachery, followed by that of Deirdre who dies from a broken heart. This legend has been dated to the first century AD.[31]

Another legend associated with the area is that of the Children of Lir, who were transformed into swans by their jealous stepmother. Condemned to spend 300 years on the Sea of Moyle, they sometimes sought shelter at the mouth of the Margy. When gales lashed the coast the swans sometimes found themselves separated, but always they were re-united at Carricknarone (the Rock of the Seals). At the end of their time on the Moyle they departed to Erris Bay in the West of Ireland where they spent another 300 years. Then one day the siblings heard a holy man ringing a bell, and at that moment they where changed back into human form. But as they were now a great age they immediately crumbled into dust.[32] Lir Integrated School, Ballycastle, was named after the Children of Lir, who remained together despite all the adversity which they encountered. There is a Lir Gardens and Lir Street in Keady, as the swans are said to have rested here on their way northwards.[33] Rathlin's wind turbines are named Aedh, Conn and Fiachra after the three sons of Lir. There is a large volume of material inspired by these tales, the best known being "Silent O Moyle" by Thomas Moore.

Prophecy:

Another Legend regarding the Pans Rocks is that the Black Nun prophesied that a red haired clergyman would one day drown here. Fr James McCann, a curate of the Ramoan Parish, was learning to swim at the Pans Rocks. One day when he had been in the water only a short time he got into difficulties. The Parish Priest of Carey, Father Eardley, who was near by dived in fully clothed, in a rescue attempt. He caught Fr McCann under his arms but there was no response - the young curate was lifeless. Dan Lamont who was also present gave assistance, risking his own life. A post-mortem was carried out in the Parochial House by Dr McElroy, Ballycastle, with J.P. O'Kane, magistrate in attendance. Cause of death was diagnosed as a heart attack,[34] yet the inscription on the headstone states otherwise. Fr McCann's remains were interred in St Patrick and St Brigid's churchyard, Ballycastle, where a Celtic Cross marks his last resting place. The inscription reads,

I.H.S
OF YOUR CHARITY
PRAY FOR
FATHER JAMES M^cCANN,
C.C. BALLYCASTLE,
WHO WAS DROWNED WHILE BATHING
ON THE 14TH OCT 1907,
THIS MEMORIAL WAS ERECTED BY THOSE
WHO KNEW AND LOVED HIM AS A GOOD
PRIEST AND TRUE SOULED IRISHMAN

beannacht De le na anam.

Rev James McCann CC Ramoan, photographed in
Coghlan's Studios, Ballycastle

John Clarke (Benmore) composed a 22 verse poem on the young priest who on the morning of his death had attended Glenshesk Chapel. The poem is entitled,

IN MEMORIAM
REV. FATHER McCANN C.C.
DROWNED AT BALLYCASTLE
14TH October, 1907.

Here again the cause of death is given as drowning as foretold by the Black Nun centuries earlier.

"And the sagart* sped on through the sedgy** glen,
As the sun climed over the hill
To flood with gold the rolling stream
The abbey, the raths and the mill."[35]

* Priest   ** Glenshesk

John Clarke
"BENMORE."
Born 11th August, 1868.

The Black Nun

Sheila Dubh McQuillan was a recluse who is said to have died about 1680.[36] Her Christian name was anglicised Julia, and Dubh, meaning black, probably described her hair colouring as a young woman. In later years, however, Dubh may have referred to the colour of her clothing and also to her supposed dabbling in the black arts. When Bonamargy was abandoned by the Franciscans, Sheila Dubh became a resident of the small gatehouse there. As the McQuillans claimed to have established the friary, Sheila Dubh must have felt that she was the rightful heir. She may have even been a member of the Franciscan Third Order which consisted of lay people, both male and female. The latter appear to have been regarded as nuns by the local populace.

Ancient holed cross, recently damaged, Bonamargy

Ann McGarry of Finvoy Parish is said to have entered the Franciscan community at Bonamargy, remaining there until the order had dispersed. Afterwards she retired to an artificial island at the Vow, where a ferry piled across the River Bann. She was described as "a nun, almost as famous for her sanctity and predictions as the Black Nun of Bonymargy".[37] This account written c1814 illustrates the Black Nun's fame at this period, and it also shows that the lay women were regarded as nuns. The Rev. George Hill (1810- 1900) wrote the following some 145 years ago.

"Many of her prophesies still float about the hill-sides and in the glens. Among her alarming predictions, she foretold the bursting of Knocklayde, and the consequent inundation of the surrounding country to the extent of seven miles".

Another prophecy is that immediately previous to that awful and extraordinary crisis which will consign Ireland exclusively and for ever to the Irish, a ship will enter the Bay of Ballycastle, with her sails on fire.[38] According to some there where seven prophesies, others say there were 21. But it is now impossible to separate the original predictions from what may be later additions.

The late Andy McKinley, Ballycastle, believed that there were 21 and he quoted the following examples. One day the large cap stone over the Grey Man's Path would fall on a ginger haired man who would be an only son. One day a coat would be hung on the Margy Bridge, and no one would be able to lift it for two years (Does this refer to a contaminated coat which will in some way cause the bridge to be sealed off for two years?). One day an iron horse will run between Ballycastle and Ballymoney. This came to pass when a Narrow Gauge Railway was opened in 1870, connecting the two towns. One day a standing stone in Carey would be married to one in Ramoan Parish. This occurred c1740 when a stone from near Culfeightrin Church and another from Woodsides farm, Carnduff, were placed beside each other in Ballycastle harbour.[39] Another prophecy was that one day Knocklayde would be spread all over Ireland. This is interpreted as referring to the Capecastle Limework's lime being spread over a wide area.[40]

She predicted that without any sign of warning the mountain of Knocklayde would burst, the surrounding country became flooded and everything destroyed for a distance of seven miles around.[41] Some have interpreted this to the supply of mains water from a reservoir on the slopes of Knocklayde. But this public utility did not cause any wide spread damage, which would seem to rule out this particular prediction. Others take the view that the last two prophesies were originally one, which had become distorted over the centuries. Julia McQuillan is credited with having forecast air travel and that men would speak to each other across the sea. A prophecy yet to be fulfilled is that the sea would return to where it had been before.[42]

Another forecast showing every indication of being fulfilled is that one day the centre of Ballycastle will be at the foot of Leyland[43] (Market Street, Ramoan Road, Leyland Road cross roads). One prophecy which has been borne out is that there would be a belt around Ireland. This has been interpreted as referring to the network of telegraph wires, phone lines and electricity cables which cover the country.[44] Another prophecy was that when trees on either side of the Quay Road branched over and met, then horse-less carriages would pass underneath. When Marconi arrived in Ballycastle in 1898, his car was one of the first ever seen in the area.[45] Photos of this period show that the trees in the area of 2 Quay Road has indeed met over head. These have since been removed. Besides her prophecies there are a number of stories told regarding Julia McQuillan. She is said to have written a letter to the Pope, who fainted upon reading it.[46] If such a letter was sent, then possibly it has survived, filed away in the Vatican archives. The coachman to a local landlord, is said to have gone around spreading false allegations regarding the Black Nun. Word of this eventually reached the man's landlord, who was so concerned that he decided to visit Bonamargy and speak to Julia. He told her what he had heard and she replied that the man would not be spreading any more lies about her. She added that the man would be in the stables when her visitor returned home. On entering the premises he found the lifeless body of the coachman hanging from a beam.[47] The best known story regarding the Black Nun is of her funeral arrangements. She left instructions that she was to be buried in a shroud, without a coffin. The spot that she chose was just inside the doorway of the west gable, so that all who entered would tread on her grave.[48] Afterwards a small, ancient, holed cross was erected on the site, but there is no information on who carried this out. The Black Nun is commemorated by the verse, entitled, "The Black Nun of Bona - Margy", composed by Samuel K. Cowan.[49]

Only a few years after Fr McCann's death, a second cleric died nearby in tragic circumstances. The Rev. Penrose was walking on the strand when he observed three female bathers in distress and shouting for help. The elderly clergyman went to their assistance, but was swept away in the strong current, while the women survived. One was the wife of a local doctor, a second was a teacher in St. Brigid's Abbey, Ballycastle.[50] Rev. John T. Penrose, M.A. was the son of Rev. John Penrose of Woodhill, Co. Cork. He died on 2nd October, 1926 aged 72, his headstone in Cushendall states that he "gave his life while trying to save others at Ballycastle". His wife Annie, daughter of Edmund McNeill, D.L., Craigdun, Co. Antrim, died 10th March 1933.

The Pans Rocks have long been a popular recreation area for local people and visitors. An early 20th century guide remarks, "The best bathing is to be had at the rocks near Bath Lodge. The gentlemen's place is approached by a wooden bridge, the ladies place is close by, and it's Crab's hole is suitable for children and ladies who can not swim. Many bathers avail themselves of the neighbouring cottage and dress there by arrangement with the owner."[51]

Previous to the erection of a foot bridge, the spot was reached by crossing over on stepping stones, at low tide. The stones ran at an angle from a point East of the present bridge. Although marked by a line of iron rails, this must have been a dangerous crossing point, especially at night, or against an incoming tide.

Pre-War recreation at the Pans Rock

One man who fished regularly at the Pans in the stepping stones era was Robert Richardson, a teacher at Ramoan National School.[52]

In 1931 the Pans Rocks Swimming Club was formed, bathing boxes were erected and diving boards were put in position.[53] The Pans was a popular pre-war venue, with large crowds assembling on Sundays to watch the dives and stunts. A favourite entertainer was Joe McPeak, famed for his impressions of Charlie Chaplin. Joe was ambitious, he emigrated to America but was killed in an accident a short time after arriving there.[54]

The question of mixed bathing and changing facilities exercised the minds of the Ballycastle Rural District Council in June, 1934. They made eight recommendations;

1. That Mr Neal Dallat be instructed to have the springboards erected
2. That the shelter erected for ladies in the east side of the rocks be removed and placed in a position adjoining the present bathing-box on the opposite side
3. That these boxes be used by ladies only
4. That Mr Bradshaw C.E. be instructed to submit sketch of a suitable shelter for men at the place usually occupied by them, with an estimate of cost of same
5. That the caretaker be instructed to see that the shelters provided and to be provided are used for dressing and undressing
6. That undressing on the rocks of adjoining strand be prohibited as well as mixed sun-bathing
7. That ladies when finished bathing be required to return to their shelter on the west side of the rocks
8. If these suggestions are not carried out in their entirety during the present season, arrangements be made for the adoption of bye-laws

under section 92 of the Public Health Acts Amended Act 1907.[55]

In the 18th Century there was a small quay at the Pans, but nothing of the structure remains today.[56] On the 19th June 1790 the sloop Ann home port Larne was lost off the Pans with the loss of two lives.[57] At this period the area was a centre for smuggling operations, and was constantly patrolled by the authorities. A close watch was kept on vessels entering and leaving Ballycastle Bay especially after the 1798 rebellion. John Curry was a United Irishman from Tonduff, near the Giant's Causeway, who was on the run after the Battle of Antrim. After a number of close escapes from the Yeomanry he reached the Pan's Rocks, where plans were carefully executed and he escaped to Boston.[58]

Salt

The Pans Rocks take their name from the ancient salt pans situated here, one of at least three locations in Carey. The saltworks are mentioned in the will of Randal MacDonnell, Earl of Antrim in 1629.[59] In the 18th century salt was manufactured elsewhere in Co. Antrim at Ballintoy, Portballintrae, Portrush, Glenarm and Larne. An early mention of the Pan's Rocks saltworks occurs during the 1641 Rebellion when William Irwin and his wife were robbed there.[60] Later in 1669 John Sharpe, Thomas Sharpe and Don Stewart are recorded as tenants.[61] There were also Stewart involvements with the saltpans at Ballintoy and Portrush.

Section of the 18th century wrought iron saltpan
Photo by Danny McGill

Local tradition is that salt from the Pan's Rocks was sent to somewhere near Glasgow, on the saltboat, an old sailing ship, which had a crew of three.[62] Records for 1738-1739 show that 30 barrels of salt went to Easdale in Scotland, and in the same period 10,090 slates were imported from Easdale.[63] In 1788 salt was sold to vessels at 45 shillings (£2.25) per ton. R. O'Mullan was paid £8.15-0 (£8.75) for making 75 tons of salt.[64]

O'Mullan Family

In the 1734 census there was a single household of the name in Culfeightrin Parish, that of Patrick O'Mullan at Bonamargy. Although he is listed as Established church,[65] there are no O'Mullans listed in 17400, which was a Protestant only census. The explanation may be that the family were nominally Protestant at the time. They were resident at Broughanlea for many years, and their burial place was Bonamargy. William O'Mullan, Broughanlea, died 4th July, 1800. Patrick O'Mullan died 23rd August, 1798, aged 33. He was buried with two of his children, although no other details were given, he appears to have been from Broughanlea. The adjacent stone is inscribed;

> A Burying Place
> For Robert O Mullan
> And family of brough
> anlea: Feby 18th 1819.

William O'Mullan farmed 21 acres at Broughanlea,[66] he died 14th October 1873, aged 89. His wife Anne died 1st March 1869, aged 78. A daughter Anne died 12th July 1882, aged 22 and son James died 28th February 1909, aged 83. This family's burial place was at Culfeightrin. At Carnduff in Ramoan Parish was another family who buried at Bonamargy. John O'Mullan died 30th June 1835, his wife Margaret died 6th December 1847, and a daughter Rose died 25th September 1865. Another daughter Margaret died 14th July 1882, and her sister Sarah died 4th August 1888. The headstone was erected by James and John, sons of John and Margaret. In 1860 James held 19 acres and 35 perches at Carnduff.[67] Their farm lay on the sea-ward side of the Back Lane and is recalled for its spring well. A local woman who was dying of cancer many years ago made one request, and that was for a bottle of water from this well.[68] There were a number of O'Mullan families in the Ballycastle area in the 18th century, but their relationship with the Broughanlea family is unknown. In Old Ramoan there is a headstone to a John O'Mullan who died 24th April 1702 aged 23.

The same graveyard contains a 19th century headstone to a Mullan family of Drummans, on the slopes of Knocklayde. Many of these Mullan and O'Mullan families have now died out.

Fever Hospital

The 1814 Rent Roll of the Ballycastle Estate records Mr Magawley as the proprietor of the Salt Works at an annual rent of £134-12-10 (approximately £134.66). He was here in 1817, but salt production must have ceased soon afterwards.[69]

A small fever hospital was established in the former saltworks with provision for 11 patients in 1823. This facility operated for only a short period.[70] A local story was that the bodies of fever victims were thrown into the near by Devil's Churn, but there is no evidence for this.[71]

Through this fearsome, subterranean cavern on the edge of the rock, the sea rushes constantly churning the water. A local man observed on a walk in 1987 that ledges and steps had been cut into the rock above the churn. But the big question was who had cut these features and for what purpose? He concluded that there had been a platform directly over the Churn, where one could stand and draw up the sea water in buckets. There is also evidence of a hatch to close off the open side, which would have provided a measure of safety. Salt was produced here by filling a saltpan with salt water and heating it until crystallisation occurred. By taking the measurements of the pan, it was calculated that approximately 2,500 gallons were required. This meant a person making over 600 trips carrying two, two gallon bucketfuls each time.

The Pans tunnel entrance with concrete path on left

Near the churn is a flight of steps which leads to a man made chamber measuring five and a half feet in height. Who executed the chamber and steps is not known, and strangely it has never had a name.

Prior to 1987 the chamber was choked with sand, which prevented any investigation of the length and direction of the chamber. That summer five people began the process of clearing the sand, but it proved a monumental task and was abandoned. The five were Danny and Jayne McGill, with their sons Andrew and Paul, and myself. Mr Padraig McCaughan, Manager of the Ballycastle ACE Scheme, was then approached and agreed to assist by providing two of his work force. The men spent a week on one of their more unusual projects. The empty chamber was five feet six inches high, 13 yards long and it did end at the side of the Churn (but the rock had not been cut through).

The discovery had left the access to the Churn theory unresolved. Was the undertaking considered too dangerous at the last moment and abandoned? The enigma of the Pans Rock remains. To the rear of the house, appropriately named "Saltpans", is a wrought iron pan, 20 feet by 16 and from 15 to 18 inches in depth.[72] There were originally two saltpans in situ, but by the time of the Rev. Richardson's visit a century ago only one remained.[73] The saltpan lies broken, half buried under debris and exposed to the elements. This unique relic of our industrial heritage is deserving of official recognition and protection. It has survived against all odds from the 1720's.

The Mines

The Ballycastle Coalfield is divided by dykes into a number of blocks, each forming separate collieries. The block nearest Ballycastle, the Saltpans Colliery lies within Broughanlea townland. An approximate guide is, from the two large black rocks on the strand to near the White Mine. Hugh Boyd (1690-1765) opened new pits here, after he gained control of the coalfield in 1736[74] The coal was used to heat the sea water in the salt pans, hence the name of the colliery. There were at least ten mines in this section but not all their names have survived.[75] The exact location of a number of the old workings are now forgotten as they were closed up due to safety considerations. For an industry that once employed hundreds, directly and indirectly, comparatively little is known. What follows is a brief outline of selected mines.

James Williamson surveyed the coalfield in 1787, his map shows a mine entrance below the road near Bath Lodge. This is the Gurdon Shaft Pit[76] but the name has never been explained. The best suggestion is that an earlier map which was inscribed Gordon (or Garden) Shaft Pit was misread.[77] There was an earlier map, but there was no known Gordon involvement with the mines at this period. A short distance east of the pit, and again below the road, the 1787 map shows an Airshaft, "worked in the 1760".[78]

The late Hugh A. Boyd knew of two mines in this area, one underneath the blue door of a shed at No. 22. This is a cottage adjacent to the right-of-way to the Pans. The second at the rear of the adjacent house "Saltpans" was once used as a cesspit. As a young boy Hugh A. was warned never to play near this spot. Between 1749- 1760, of the five pits worked in the Saltpans Colliery, four were just above high water level.[79] Above the road was the Engine Pit, as shown in the 1787 map with coal at 45yards, and the seam from 6-9 feet thick.[80]

This mine was worked below sea level, the water was pumped out by a water powered wheel, similar to a mill wheel. The water was conveyed all the way from the Carey River, over a mile distant. The aqueduct, constructed by Boyd was approximately five yards wide, and it usually gave a plentiful supply of water. The wheel had fallen into a state of disrepair by 1784, and the mine had ceased working.

A sketch of this watercourse may yet be seen around the Doon and to the rear of 7 Carrickmore Road. The watercourse ends in the rough patch of ground behind No. 11. Local tradition regarding the Engine Pit is that it was also knon as the Saltpans Mine, as its coal was used at the Saltpans.[81] This is despite the fact that it was not the mine nearest the pans, and it had closed by1784, years before salt production had ceased. The Sliding Shaft Pit, No.2 on the 1787 map, was East of the Gurdon Shaft Pit, and was being worked in 1749.[82] There were a number of pits in this general area, one survived into the early years of the 20th century. A cutting dated 3rd July 1899 gives the following account. *"The mines latterly have been altogether neglected. There is another start being made to open these mines, and the party (a field club) found a steam engine in full work clearing the shaft of the mine not far from Bath Lodge preparatory to further work"*.

Another cutting from Robert McCahan's scrapbooks advertises a three ton weighbridge to be sold at the Bath Lodge Pit by auction in April 1910. At the rear of No.15 is a bricked up mine entrance, with scum oozing out near-by.[83] In the general area of "Kilcraig", there were four mines marked on the O.S. Maps of the 1830's. On the road below is a small lay-by and during its construction a pillar of coal was discovered. The late Jamie Davidson, who worked on the lay-by, recalled obtaining a couple of bags of coal. He was a former miner, and he explained that this was known as "robbing" the pillar.[84]

Locals from Ballycastle regularly went around to the Pans area to hoke coal for domestic use. One man was Dickie Duffin, and when he had obtained a sufficient quantity, he placed the bag of coal on his bike and cycled home.[85] The late Tom McGuile, Ballycastle, hoked coal at a spot near the White Mine, and the late Jackie Dillon, Ballycastle, recalled hoking coal around the shore with another man, in the late 1950's. When they had filled three bags or so, arrangements were then made to transport the coal home. Payment was a few shillings to cover the cost of the petrol. This coal was described as being of poor quality, and more like slate.[86]

Around the bend in the road from the lay-by is Poulnageeragh, No. 5 on the 1787 map. These old workings are hidden away from view and few people know of their existence.

Poulnageeragh mine entrance in Spring time

Three entrances can be discovered about half way up the cliff, one is almost obscured by a jumble of rocks. Two are on the same level, a larger and higher entrance may have been an airway. Dickie Duffin, a former miner, knew nothing of the history of these mines, only that the coal seams here were the Hawk's Nest and Splint Coal.[87]

As there is no evidence of a roadway, and the ground is quite steep, the coal must have been tipped down wooden chutes to the road. The name Poolnageeragh means either the pits of the sheep, or pits of the thicket (Puil na Gaertha). Before the construction of the road this sheltered spot would have formed a natural shrubbery. This area marks the Eastern boundry of the Saltpans Colliery. Along the road at Poolnageeragh there were two springs, but today only one is to be seen. The larger one provided a fresh water supply for horses, while at the second spring the men quenched their thirst.

Jamie McDonnell, Jim McAuley and Willie McMullan (Ramoan Road) watered their horses here when they were carting clinker from the Iron Stage area in 1937.[88] At a gap in the road-side wall there is a ramp (now largely over grown) down to the shore. This is Port Watty, which the old residents pronounced Portavatty.[89]

Remains of the ramp below Poulnageeragh

A short distance past the gap in the roadside wall is a recess, where the line of the road changes abruptly. There appears to have been a roadway or ramp leading down to the shore. This would have facilitated a one-way system for horses and carts using one ramp when loaded, and returning empty by the second route.

Old section of roadway at Poulnageeragh

Some years ago Danny McGill noted a relatively level area on the shore between the ramps, but there is no evidence of a pier. Perhaps the coal was loaded at the waters edge into small boats, which then supplied larger vessels in deep water. Such a system, while labour intensive and more expensive, is known to have been used at some Collieries. On a sea facing, rock ledge a shallow but uneven channel has been cut. There is no obvious purpose for the channel, it may have never been completed. What was going on here remains a mystery.

Billy's Shank

East of the ramps, where the sea laps against the base of the wall, is a very narrow adit called Billy's Shank.

This was not only an airway to the White Mine, but it was also in theory an escape route, despite the fact that it is below High Water Level. The adit was also where the pumps emptied the water from the colliery in a vain attempt to keep the mine dry. Dick Duffin (Dickie's father) and Dan McKiernan, Tornaroan, were two men who manned the pumps at different periods. As a boy during World War I, Dickie Duffin occasionally walked up to McQuilkin's farm at Tornabodagh to obtain fresh buttermilk. He recalled looking over the wall at Billy's Shank and watching Johnny Kerrigan working the pumps.[90] A grill placed across the entrance now prevents access to the old adit.

The White Mine was opened by Hugh Boyd some time after he gained control of the coalfield in 1736. Williamson's map records the mine as No. 6, with coal at 26 yards.[91] The seam worked here was the Main Coal, which lies below sea level, hence the constant flooding. Below the coal lies a layer of white sandstone glistening in the wet conditions. This is the feature which gives the mine it unusual name.[92]

The White Mine - Photo by Danny McGill

Situated in Broughanlea townland, in 1860 the mine was held in fee by the representatives of Hugh Boyd, at an annual Valuation of £30.[93]

The Ballycastle Development Limited was incorporated in April 1897 with a capital of £2,000 in £1 shares. They acquired the mining rights on the Boyd Estate, and installed machinery for pumping the mine. Although the steam pumps were kept operating day and night, they failed to control the flow of water, and the company were forced to abandon the mine. The Belfast Coal & Iron Limited formed in July 1906, attempted working the mine, but their steam pump was not powerful enough to control the volume of water and they too abandoned operations. Their plant and machinery was sold off in July 1908.

A new company was then formed, the Ballycastle M֮ Syndicate Limited, with an office in Glasgow. They were work White Mine in May 1912, but ceased after the death of their chֈ promoter.[94] The mine had a checkered history, worked for a periou abandoned, the re-opened in another spasm of activity. There were number of coal faces within the white mine, each worked by an indi miner.

Denis Kerr, Tornabodagh, was a miner who was better known as Denis Carr. Another two Carey miners were Ned Hill, who died in 1963, and Arthur Stewart who lived at Colliers Row, Ballyreagh. Dick and George Caulfield were clerks in the office, which was located at the front of the mine entrance. The sandstone building was kept whitewashed, but eventually became a ruin and was demolished in the 1980's. A toilet block now occupies this site. Alex Butler was a shoemaker, widely known as Waxey, and he was a night watchman for a time. Tom Greer, Drumawillan, father of the late Dick Greer, was a ganger.[95] Mick McAuley, Carey Mill, was the night watchman here in 1948.

The nightwatchman's hut at the 'white mine' was a popular location for people to ceilidh on winter nights. Jim Fogarty, Tom Greer, Mick Rooney & Seamus Clarke were regulars on Sunday evenings. Jack McMichael and "Bounder" McHenry were occasional visitors who are recalled.[96] The pumps in the mine were prone to problems because of the damage caused by the salt water. Application was made for Government aid, similar to what the German mines received, but this was turned down.[97] The late Dan Duncan, Tornabodagh, recalled exploring the mine. He described the supporting timbers of oak as being about 18 inches thick and extremely hard. When he attempted to stick his pen knife in the wood, all he managed to achieve was to scratch the surface.[98] In the final years of the mine the coal was winched to the surface, but previously ponies had been used to haul the coal ladened bogies up the steep incline. At night the animals were stabled near the mine entrance, and there was once a smithy located here.[99]

About 1950 John McCracken, who had been involved with an Ayrshire mine, came over an obtained a lease from Lord Antrim to work the White Mine. John's father was a native of Dunloy, who had left the family farm in 1910 to seek work in Scotland. John's two nephews, James and his twin brother Willie, joined their uncle in the enterprise. The latter recalls the day that he and Ned Hill were engulfed by a seam of sand which suddenly poured through the roof of the mine. They managed to escape and the breach was eventually sealed again.

There was another incident when a shot prepared for blasting failed to go off, and the men re-entered the mine without waiting the obligatory 30 minutes. A new shot was then prepared and the men had just retreated a short distance when the original shot went off. Although they felt the force of the blast, the men escaped without injury. Part of the mine suffered from a poor supply of air, and when John McCracken lit a candle, it went out. The miners discovered a seven foot seam of coal but they soon came upon a "hitch", a fault which altered everything.[100] The pumps were operated by Lawrence McHenry, Ballyvoy, pumping out approximately 600 gallons per minute, but it was a losing battle. The massive coal pillars which supported the roof of the mine were "robbed" and the White Mine was abandoned for the final time.[101]

Percy French (1854 -1920) performed at a concert in the Masonic Hall about 1917. The late Hugh A Boyd recalled missing the show as he did not have sufficient pocket money at the time. He also recalled that on the door of the former office at the White Mine, there was a poster advertising the concert. For a number of years, after the death of Percy French, the poster remained reminding Hugh A of what he had missed.[102]

The area beside the old building was used regularly by campers. One group of horse dealers would arrive in the summer and stay for a few weeks, or even a couple of months. They travelled in two horse drawn caravans. The women sold combs, needles and other small items. Dickie Duffin taught the men how to fish and afterwards they spent their evenings at the Pans fishing.[103] Another group named Roach, who were from the South of Ireland, camped for a period in the 1930's at the White Mine.[104] Today this ground at the entrance to the White Mine is an official camping site, part of the Maguires Strand Caravan Park.

Falbane Colliery

Williamson's 1787 map gives 2 mines below the road, east of the White Mine. No 7 is simply marked Pit and No 8 The Scythe-stone house level, with coal at 160 yards. These mines were on either side of a dyke which crosses the foreshore at an angle.[105] The No 7 pit is shown on the first map, but little else is known of its history. It formed part of the Falbane Colliery, which takes its name from fál meaning a wall or ditch, and bán, white. Today there is no trace of any wall of white sandstone material which no doubt came from the White Mine quarry. Pit no 8 takes its name from a nearby house which had some association with the production of scythe-stones.

This old established industry produced scythe-stones in vast numbers. Larger and heavier than a modern stone they were used for sharpening tools mainly scythes. The white sandstone was found to be the best suited for this purpose, and a skibbling tool was used their manufacture. By 1741 Ballycastle scythe-stones were being advertised in the Freeman's Journal, Dublin.[106] But they must have been used centuries earlier as revealed by an excavation of the base of Armoy Round Tower. Here a portion of sandstone was found which archaeologists identified as having been used for whetting the workers tools.[107]

An 1812 report states that the scythe-stones were sold by the dozen in hardware shops throughout the neighboring counties.[108] This forgotten industry was still operating in the 1850's but had ceased by the end of the century. The late Pat McBride, Ballyreagh, told how scythe-stones were made on a casual basis at the Iron Stage. A channel was cut in the rock, and then a rough block of sandstone was inserted and rolled continuously until the required shape had been achieved.[109] Another local resident heard of the same method being employed at Carrickmore. He decided to experiment and made a few sharpening stones, but declared that it was too time consuming and certainly not worth the bother.[110] From time to time, the old Ballycastle scythe-stones are discovered in various locations. One was discovered during the renovation of a house near Plumfall in the 1980's[111] and another was found in a bog at The Drones, Loughguile.[112] The local sandstone was used to produce a wide range of products, which are discussed in Chapter Two.

The seam worked at the Scythestone House Level was the main coal which had been worked out by the 1830's. On the slope below Corrymeela there were a number of small mines. One was the Falbane Adit, which was recorded in 1817, with coal at 160 yards.[113] By April, 1899 Falbane Colliery had ceased working. A report for the year ending 31/12/1898 shows the number of days worked each month and the amount of coal extracted.[114]

January	24	July	24
February	23	August	25
March	25	September	26
April	26	October	26
May	25	November	26
June	23	December	27

Output at Falbane Colliery in 1899 was;

	Tons	Cwt	
Coal	704	16	2
Slack	805	3	0
Total	1509	19	2

A few years after Falbane had closed, a local miner who was exploring the area, discovered a good seam of coal. He worked the seam for some time before selling out to the Scottish firm, Heckie Aiton and Kerr.[115]

Corrymeela and Maguires Strand

Above Falbane is internationally renowned Corrymeela, a Christian centre which has been the subject of numerous film and radio documentaries. Corrymeela has also spawned a number of books, as the centre provided a temporary refuge for many people during the darkest days of The Troubles. Moira O'Neill's famous poem, "Corrymeela", refers not to this location but to the townland of Corrymellagh, near Cushendun.[116]

The centre was established as a Christian Fellowship hostel about 1931. Local men Dan McKiernan, Tornaroan, Bob and Paddy Lynn, Ballyvoy, worked on the construction. The Lynn brothers were stonemasons, and Bob was known over a wide area for his weather forecasts.[117]

Established in the mid 1960's the Corrymeela community has grown enormously since then. The whole site has in recent years been revamped, the original chalets were sold off, to begin a new life as garden sheds and children's houses. An Croi, which means heart, is the spiritual heart of the community, and a place of prayer and meditation. Viewed from the slope, its stone contours rise above the cliffs like a modern cashel (now screened by recent planting).

Maguires Strand

Maguire's Strand and Maguire's Bay are named after two Dublin bankers and merchants, brothers Richard and William McGwire. They leased the Ballycastle Coalfield in 1720, and this was how they signed their names. Richard McGwire was dead by 1730 and William had given up his interests in what was then a very remote area.[118]

On the Eastside of Maguire's Bay is Coyle's Rock, the site of a wooden pier, from where coal was shipped to Dublin and elsewhere. As the bay is named after the Maguires, it is likely that they constructed the pier, and had their coalyard at Maguire's Strand.

The well built sandstone boundary wall of the latter place indicated the importance of the site. A family named Maguire were residing in the Maguire's Strand house about a century ago and it is widely believed that the strand was named after them. But the place name pre-dates this family by some 160 years.

Meehan Family

Francis Meehan was the tenant here is 1860, and John McGildowny was the landlord.[119] The Meehans were a fishing family, they had little choice as they held just over one acre of land. Two Meehan brothers drowned while fishing within sight of their home, towards the end of the 19th century. It is believed that their boat struck a reef and capsized, at what was afterwards called Meehan's Bow[120] (a bow was a submerged reef). The location was noted for the large sized lythe and glashan which were caught here. Dick Duffin (father of Dickie Duffin) once caught a 17 pound lythe, just off Meehan's Bow.

A John McMeehan who died at Blackside, Knocksoghey, aged 91, in Feburary 1853, may have been a relation. The names Meehan, McMeehan and McMeekin were all considered as one, a century ago at Ballycastle. The following were recorded by Griffith c 1860; John McMicken, house and 19 acres, 3 roads and 5 perches, Ballydurnian. Patrick McMicken had a house in Clare Street with a separate yard, leased form the committee of the Wesleyan Methodist Congregation. Robert McMicken, house and 15 acres, 25 perches at Churchfield, with a further 12 acres at Bonamargy, and 9 acres, 3 roads and 10 perches at Losset.[121] The surname with it variants has now died out.

Corrymeela and Maguires Strand

The little road that starts at Maguire's Strand and climbs up past Corrymeela would have witnessed a hive of activity two and a half centuries ago. A spoil heap on the lower side of the road is still bare and raw, but on the upper side the spoil is now largely under vegetation. These mines, one was worked pre 1831, were part of Falbane Colliery in Drumaroan townland.

Tornabodagh

A basalt dyke at the end of Maguire's Strand marks the boundary of Drumaroan and Tornabodagh. The latter is from the Gaelic Tor na Bodach, the towering rock of the churl, or ignorant one.

The tor in question rises abruptly above the road, its summit crowned with an early promontory fort called Doon. The army had a look-out post here in World War Two, and when they abandoned the post it was soon colonized by briars and brambles. Locals then gave it the nickname the Crow's Nest.[122]

The level area East of the Doon has been worked for its coal since the 18th century. On the 1787 map, Tournabuddock Shaft is marked, with coal at 38 yards.[123] Until recently a mine called the Deugh (pronounced dook) was to be seen with its brick lined entrance, roofed with old railway sleepers. From its proximity to the Doon, the mine was known as the Doon Drift (a drift was a mine with more than one entrance).[124]

Heckie, Aiton and Kerr were a Scottish company established in April 1917 and in May they began work at the Deugh. They soon came upon a narrow seam of coal, which they began mining instead of leaving it to form a roof. This resulted in an enormous quantity of water and running sand from an old mine on a higher level, flooding the Deugh. The firm paid a high price for their short sighted policy as their work was impeded for almost a year.[125]

Of the company's three directors only Heckie seems to have spent much time in Ballycastle. He stayed in a house in the Warren, and it was said that he had a wooden leg. Locals who worked for Heckie included Paddy McAfee and Dan Black who were both from Ballycastle. The latter worked as a carpenter in the United States. After some years he returned home and was ever afterwards known as Yankee Dan. Ned Hill and Denis Kerr were 2 well known miners who worked at the Deugh.

Kerr Family

Denis who lived at Tornabodagh over looking the mine, emigrated to America but returned after sometime.[126] He died 15th January 1962 aged 72, and was buried at Carey Chapel. Henry McKiernan, Tornaroan, was a miner at the Deugh. He came from a family long associated with the collieries. The surname Kerr was locally pronounced as Carr. A John Kerr of Ballyvoy died 6th April 1876, aged 84, and his wife Catherine died 5th April 1875 aged 83. Their headstone in Culfeightrin Churchyard also records three sons, Henry, William and John. There was one daughter Ann but no further details are given.

A John Carr had a house with 26 acres, 2 roads and 20 perches at Ballyvoy in 1860. Mary Carr lived nearby in a small house leased off John Carr. At the same time there was a John Kerr at Davey's Row, Clare Street, Ballycastle.[127] The 1734 Census records a John Kerr at Ballyucan,[128] and in Bonamargy there is a small headstone inscribed with a coat of arms below the word SPERO.

This side of the stone is inscribed;

THIS IS YE PLACE
APPOINTED FOR
YE BURIAL OF ARTHUR
KER & HIS FAMILY

The reverse of the stone is inscribed,

+
I H S
HERE LYETH YE BODY
OF ARTHUR KER WHO
DIED NOVER YE 15TH 1738
AGED 1 YEAR

The Deugh

Book-keeping at the Deugh was done by a man named Caulfield, who operated from a wooden shed on the site. Hughie McGill was the night watchman, he had suffered a foot injury when working on the Pier Yard, Ballycastle. This left Hughie unable to undertake any heavy manual work. Hughie's wife, Cassie (nee Duffin, an aunt of Dickie Duffin), operated a private lending library in Ann Street, Ballycastle, in the 1940's. The pumps at the Deugh were kept operating 24hours a day, and part of Hughie's duties consisted of checking the pumps at regular intervals. Hughie's hut was popular with the locals who provided company for the watchman, as they spent the night playing cards.[129]

Coal from the mine sold at £2-10-0 per ton (£2.50) in July 1918. But by the following April the firm had ceased operating and all their plant and machinery was sold. Directors of the firm were Thomas C. Kerr, Chairman, John R. Aiton and John Heckie of John Heckie, Son & Company. The latter were Commission and Machinery Agents, with an office at 58 Dundas Street, Glasgow.[130]

The following account, dated 30th September 1918, from one of Robert McCahon's scrapbooks gives one reason which led to the firm pulling out. He (Heckie) had had a tremendous amount of trouble at the mine. He had suffered a strike, intimidation and boycott.

The average output per man was two tons of coal per day, but only 15 cwt was now being dug out per man, and it cost 52s 11d (approximately £2.65) to bring each ton of coal to the surface. At this period Robert Thompson, Ballycastle, was sub-manager, Robert Dunlop was the winding engine man, and the mechanic was Thomas Greer.

This was not Heckie's first legal action regarding mines as another cutting, dated February 1912, shows. The Ballycastle Mines were again the subject matter of an action brought before Mr Justice Boyd in the Dublin courts. John Heckie, Mine Manager, Ardtully Mines, Kilgarvan, Co. Kerry, brought a claim against Henry Walker, a copper chemist of Dalkey, Co. Dublin. The case concerned an agreement between Heckie and Walker which was entered into the previous July with Miss Boyd, concerning the leasing of the Ballycastle mines, and materials on the Ballycastle Estate.

One of the men brought over to install machinery at the Deugh was Collins, a Cork man who had settled in Glasgow. While working here he lodged at the farmhouse known as the Lawn (previously owned by the McCambridge family). With his work completed he went back to Glasgow, returning as often as possible for a holiday. He brought his family with him and on one occasion his son Denis met Lily Duffin, who resided in Union Street, Ballycastle. The couple eventually married and settled here, but as they had no children the name has now died out.[131]

The entrance to the Deugh was filled in a few years ago, and at present there is no indication that a mine ever existed here. The night watchman's hut is long gone, an old green caravan stood on the site in the 1960's. At the base of the cliff is a portion of wall. This was where the steam pump was positioned, enclosed by a stone wall.[132] Above the Deugh, at the rear of the Doon, is a small slag heap, and hidden below is a mine entrance.

This was opened by Dan Mc Kiernan when he was working to Jim Greer about 1948. The coal was hauled out in a wooden box, sleigh like. Dan's wife Mary (nee Duffin, Glenravel) assisted in the work on occasions. Mining operations did not last long however. When the field immediately above the mine was ploughed, there was a subsidence which resulted in the roof of the mine collapsing. The workings were then abandoned.[133]

The entrance to the Deugh was filled in a few years ago, and at present there is no indication that a mine ever existed here. The night watchman's hut is long gone, an old green caravan stood on the site in the 1960's. At the base of the cliff is a portion of wall. This was where the steam pump was positioned, enclosed by a stone wall.[132] Above the Deugh, at the rear of the Doon, is a small slag heap, and hidden below is a mine entrance. This was opened by Dan Mc

Coyles rock, wooden pier site

Kiernan when he was working to Jim Greer about 1948. The coal was hauled out in a wooden box, sleigh like. Dan's wife Mary (nee Duffin, Glenravel) assisted in the work on occasions. Mining operations did not last long however. When the field immediately above the mine was ploughed, there was a subsidence which resulted in the roof of the mine collapsing. The workings were then abandoned.[133]

Up to the 1940's there was a deeply rutted cart track to be seen on the Duncan's farm, Tornabodagh. The track which led down to the Deugh has long since been filled in to level off the ground.[134] On the same farm there was a sandstone arch, which was sealed by Denis Kerr about 60 years ago. This had been the entrance to an airway of a mine in the area, which formed part of the North Star Colliery.

The Coyle Family

Coyles Rock juts out from below the corner about 100 yards past the Deugh. There is now no tradition of who is commemorated here, the late Jack Coyle stated that it was not his family. As there was a family named Coyle residing at Tornaroan during the 19th century, they are probably the Coyles associated with the rock. They may have fished here regularly as this was once a popular fishing location with fishermen.

Fishing weight?

The family's burial place was at the front of Carey Chapel. One headstone is to Ann Coyle, wife of "Henery", who died 4th April 1841, aged 60. The adjacent stone is to another Henry Coyle, who died 6th September 1881, aged 60. A son John died 30th November 1876 aged 26. Another son Henry died in Pennsylvania, USA, 18th January 1882 aged 38. Andrew died 13th June 1893, aged 30 and Daniel died 26th June 1907, aged 65. Mary Ann, Henry's wife, died 12th December 1897 aged 75. A grandson John Coyle died 1st August 1895, aged 10 years.

There were no Coyles at Tornaroan in 1860, but at Townparks a Henry Coyle is recorded, with a Daniel Coyle at Ballyvoy.[136] Henry Coyles was a miner residing at Bath Lodge in 1863, where is son Daniel, also a miner, married Mary Darragh. She was a daughter of John, a stonecutter, and was a sister to Dan Darragh who died in 1870.

The house across the road from Coyles rock, was buil
named Hutton. Lawrence McHenry worked on its construction
recalls copper pipes being filled with sand in order to bend the
causing damage. This was the old method of bending copper pi
ever he had a spare moment Lawrence walked over to Coyles R
he fished for murrans. The plumber expressed an interest, and Li....ence
showed him the basics of rock fishing. Others who fished here included the
McGill brothers, Jim and John of Ann Street.[137] Dickie Duffin also
occasionally fished murrans here., but Francis McAllister, Drumavoley,
was a regular. Francis, who also trapped rabbits, suffered from a leg or foot
injury died in 1976.[138]

A woman named Farrell from Dundalk drowned here in 1941. She
was preparing to cook dinner and had gone out to gather driftwood, as she
did regularly. When she did not return a search was begun, Paddy Maguire,
who lived at Maguires Strand, discovered her body in shallow water. The
woman had suffered head injuries, which lead to the conclusion that she
had slipped and was knocked unconscious, before eventually drowning.[139]

Rows of postholes at Coyles Rock are evidence that a wooden pier
once existed here. Dating possibly from the 1720's, this was one of a
number of locations from which coal was sent out by sea. The late Dickie
Duffin had heard of a spot somewhere along the shore which was known
as Colliery Rock. He believes that this was the former name of Coyles
Rock. A brief article and sketch of the site by Danny McGill, appeared in
the Glynns Volume 17.

Fisher Family

Fishers Port is a little creek a few yards from the vacant house,
formerly called Union Cottage. Johnny Fisher once farmed at Tornaroan,
and he often made use of the port to which he gave his name.[140] The family
had arrived in Glenarm from Scotland during the 18th century and after
some time moved to Drumnakeel. They were shepherds at this time, by
1801 they had settled at Dunmakelter, where they remain to the present
day.[141] Thomas Fisher is recorded repairing sections of road at Ballyucan
and Dunmakelter in 1849.[142] He married Sarah McCambridge from
Glendun, 24th May 1860.

The shore from Bonamargy to Portnaloub produces a rich harvest of kelp which today is neglected, but in the past often lead to legal disputes. Many Carey farmers claimed the right to gather the kelp, and Jack Coyle (died 1999) recalled seeing boats in all the little ports, which are now deserted. All the tangles and coarse seaweeds were referred to as kelp or wrack. The Cuckoo Storms in May cast up a massive amount on the shores, and this was called the May Fleece, or the May Bulk.[143] A Carey man, who worked on numerous farms, recalled going down to the shore to gather tangles at five on a winter's morning. This was because it was a race to get there first to state your claim. The tangles were spread over a field, then chopped up with a spade and ploughed in, especially for a crop of turnips or potatoes.[144]

A Ballintoy man, hired at a young age in Carey, recalled seeing wrack drawn by horse and cart from Maguires Strand. The ancient cart road here was a right-of-way.[145] These farmers who gathered the kelp were not permitted to remove sand, gravel or any other material, nor could they burn or sell any kelp. This was a highly controlled procedure where one person might lease the shores of a number of townlands. Michael Hall, Tornaroan, leased from John McGildowny the following kelp shores c1860;

Drumaroan	Annual Valuation	£2-15-0
Tornabodagh	Annual Valuation	£2-10-0
Turnaroan	Annual Valuation	£7-0-0
Ballynaglogh	Annual Valuation	£1-0-0
Ballyvoy	Annual Valuation	£3-10-0

Total
£16-15-0 (£16,75)

He also had leased at Tornaroan a farm of 16 acres, 3 roads and 20 perches.[146] The family had been resident in the parish from at least 1734, when 3 Hall households were recorded in the census of that year.[147] Earlier an Alex Hall was recorded in Ballycastle in 1669, but in Carey there were none.[148]

Family tradition is that Michael bred horses for a Lord Annesley, but it is not know where this occurred. Michael married Ellen Knowe in 1841, and when he died in 1882, Ellen emigrated to Australia with a son Henry. At least three other children, Margaret, Ester and Sarah-Jane, emigrated to Australia or New Zealand. Esther is known to have married a John O'Hara, but of the five siblings left behind in Tornaroan, nothing is known.[149] Today the name Hall has died out and is virtually forgotten.

The kelp shores of Bonamargy and Broughanlea on the Boyd Estate c 1860 were leased by John McDonnell from the Representatives of Hugh Boyd. Patrick Scully (Scally) leased the kelp shores of Ballyreagh Lower from Alex McCambridge, who in turn held the lease from the representatives of Hugh Boyd.[150] The kelp shores of Cross and Ballyreagh Upper are not recorded in Griffith's Valuation. The latter townland which includes Fairhead, is inaccessible for kelp gathering.

Jamie Harrigan, Broughanlea, and Jamie McAuley, Carvadoon Cottages, both burned kelp in large quantities, the latter at Carrickmore.[151] Francis Maguire, Maguire's Strand,[152] and Paddy Glenfield, Ballyvoy, were two others, the latter burned his kelp near the Iron Stage. John McNally and Jim McAuley also burned kelp in this area when they lived in Carey. They also burned kelp at the North Star Dyke.[153]

The late Dan Duncan, Tornabodagh, recalled once going down with a horse and slipe (a simple A-shaped wooden frame used for drawing loads where carts were unsuited) to gather a load of kelp. He had collected a good load when a North-Westerly struck, and suddenly everything was in the water. By good fortune Dan was deposited at the back of his horse, which he clung to and safely got back on shore. The load of kelp was lost, washed away and all his hard work had been in vain, but he had been lucky.[154]

The gathering and burning of kelp was a cottage industry which has now passed into folk lore. Robert McMullan the Portballintrae poet, "North Antrim", published a volume of his poetry in 1933. The late Jamie Brennan, North Street, Ballycastle, lent me his copy which he had received from his son in New Zealand. He had discovered the book in a second hand bookshop, after noting that a previous owner had penciled in the names of people featured in photographs. One of the poems was entitled, "Burning the Kelp", and others were "Tangle Dulse" and "The Dulse Gatherer". "Sea Wrack", a poem by Moira O'Neill appears in "Songs of the Glens of Antrim".

Burning kelp was hot, dirty work and involved large volumes of smoke which was said to bring rain. When kelp was burned in Rathlin, even at night, Ballycastle people could tell from the reek which carried for many miles.[155] A common remark around Carnlough was "The kelp is shining on you", which referred to new clothes bought as a result of kelp burning.[156]

Locals are sometimes surprised to hear dulse being referred to as dulisk at the Lammas Fair, but both words are from the Gaelic duilisc. A traditional song reguarding dulse, "Dúlamán na Binne Bui", comes from Omeath, Co. Louth. Around Benvan the Gaelic for edible seaweeds was cnaosach, while the dulse hook was called a corran cnaosaigh.[157]

North Star Dyke

Between Coyles Rock and the North Star Dyke are a number of small adits, hidden from view, and also from recorded history.

North Star Dyke

The North Star Dyke is a well known local landmark of black basalt which points northwards, hence its name. Earlier the dyke was called Cassanbarra (Caskinbarrow on some maps), which means Barach's path. He was the legendary chieftain of Torr, who had a central role in the Exile of the Children of Uisneach.[158] From a height the dyke with its regular width appears to be a footpath running in to the sea. This was a natural pier, accessible even at low water.[159] The Belfast artist Joseph W. Carey illustrated this in 1896, when he sketched a boat pushing off from the dyke to fish. This painting with three others of Carey's may be viewed in Ballycastle Museum. There is also in the Boyd Arms, Ballycastle, a photo showing a boat inscribed "Captain", beached beside the North Star Dyke.

Finally there is place name evidence, the area immediately east of the dyke was known as Tornaroan Port.[160] The little bay is Colliery Bay, but this name now appears to be no longer in use.

Chapter One, References.

1. Place-Names of Northern Ireland, Volume Seven, p9 edited by Fiachra Mac Gabhann, Q.U.B. 1997.
2. The Life of Barney Maglone, pp1,7, McCahan's Local Histories, Glens of Antrim Historical Society, 1988.
3. Place-Names of Northern Ireland, Volume Seven, p127
4. Maureen Morgan, Ballycastle
5. Dickie Duffin (deceased) Ballycastle
6. Hugh A. Boyd (deceased) Ballycastle
7. Seamus Clarke (deceased) Ballycastle
8. Glynns Vol 19, p44
9. Seamus Clarke
10. Hugh A. Boyd
11. Hugh A. Boyd, Dickie Duffin
12. Mickie McGuile (deceased) Ballycastle
13. Chronicle, 4/5/1985
14. Dickie Duffin
15. Seamus Clarke
16. Glynns Vol 5, p7
17. John Humphreys, Ballycastle
18. James McMichael (deceased) Ballycastle, who was informed by his father.
19. Jack Coyles (deceased) Ballycastle
20. Dickie Duffin
21. History of Ballycastle, p2, McCahan's Local Histories
22. Andy McKinley (deceased) Ballycastle , Dickie Duffin
23. Slater's Directory. p27
24. Seamus Clarke
25. Dickie Duffin
26. Seamus Clarke
27. Glynns Vol 1, p13
28. Bun-Na-Margie, p45, Francis Joseph Bigger U.J.A. 1898
29. Thoughts From The Heart, by Benmore, Irish News Ltd. Belfast, 1908 and M.H.Gill & Sons, Dublin.
30. Glynns Vol 4, pp25, 29
31. The Macdonnells of Antrim, pp 8, 24, by George Hill. Reprint, Glens Of Antrim Historical Society, Ballycastle, 1976
32. Ballycastle Guide, p8 J.S. Scarlett, Ballycastle. n.d.
33. R. Ulster programme

34. The Glensman, February 1932, p3
35. Blossoms from the Hedgerows, p61 by Benmore, W & G Baird, Belfast, and M.H.Gill & Sons, Dublin. n.d.
36. Dr Cahal Dallat
37. Parochial Survey of Ireland. Volume One, p382. The account of Finvoy Parish is by Rev. James Grier.
38. Ulster Journal of Archaeology, Volume 8, p21, 1860.
39. Andy McKinley and others
40. Dickie Duffin
41. Bunnamairge Friary, p11. McCahon's local Histories
42. Coleraine Tribune. 3/7/1985, article by Dr Cahal Dallat
43. Frank McCormick, Portrush who was informed by his father. The McCormicks lived in a house near the crossroads.
44. Dickie Duffin
45. Charlie McAfee (deceased) Moyle Road, Ballycastle and David Dillon
46. Joe Keenan (deceased) Ballycastle
47. Ellen O'Kane (deceased) Ballycastle, who was informed by her father Jim McAuley
48. Dickie Duffin and others
49. Idylls of Ireland, p34, Marcus Ward & Company third edition 1896
50. Hugh A Boyd and Seamus Clarke
51 A Guide to Ballycastle And Neighbourhood, p101. Rev. Alfred Richardson, 1905
52. Jamie McKiernan, (deceased) Ballycastle
53. Hugh A. Boyd
54. Dickie Duffin
55. Northern Constitution, 16/6/1934, obtained from Nevin Taggart, Magherintendry.
56. Danny McGill, Ballinlea
57. Shipwrecks Of The Ulster Coast, p145, by Ian Wilson, Impact – Amergin, Coleraine, 1979
58. Tales From The Glens Of Antrim, p4, McCahan's Local Histories
59. Glynns Vol 16, p17
60. Coleraine Tribune. 6/3/1985
61. Glynns Vol 1, p15
62. Dickie Duffin
63. The Rise and Decline of The Ballycastle Coalfield and Associated Industries, 1720-1840, p184. M.A. Thesis by George A.Wilson, Q.U.B. 1951

64. The Causeway Coast, p159, J.E.Mullin, B.A. second edition, 1982.
65. Glynns Vol 21 p71
66. Griffith Valuation, p56
67. Griffith Valuation, p60
68. Mary McAuley (deceased), Kenbane
69. Ballycastle Estate records, held by Greer, Hamilton & Gailey, Ballymoney.
70. Dr Cahal Dallat
71. Dickie Duffin
72. Danny McGill, Ballinlea; see Glynns Vol 16, pp17-21 and Glynns Vol 17, p27 for local salt making.
73. Richardson p14
74. Geology of North Antrim p73, McCahan's Local Histories
75. Dickie Duffin
76. Geology Of North Antrim, p6
77. Danny McGill
78. Geology Of North Antrim, p6
79. Undated cuttings, McCahan's scrapbook
80. Geology Of North Antrim, p6
81. Dickie Duffin
82. Geology Of North Antrim, p6
83. Peter Montgomery, Ballycastle
84. Jamie Davidson, Ballycastle, died 7/12/2004
85. Neil Connor, Ballycastle
86. Jackie Dillon
87. Dickie Duffin
88. John McAuley, Manchester formerly of Carey
89. Jack Coyles and Dickie Duffin
90. Dickie Duffin
91. Geology of North Antrim, pp 3,6.
92. Dickie Duffin
93. Griffith Valuation, p56
94. Geology Of North Antrim, p11
95. Dickie Duffin
96. John McAuley, Manchester and Seamus Clarke
97. Andy McKinley (deceased)
98. Dan Duncan (deceased)
99. Dickie Duffin
100. Willie McCracken, Ballymoney
101. Lawrence McHenry, Ballyvoy
102. Hugh A. Boyd

103. Dickie Duffin
104. John McAuley, Manchester
105. McCahan's Local Histories
106. The Rise and Decline of The Ballycastle Coalfield and Associated Industries 1720 – 1840
107. Ulster Journal of Archaeology, Vol 4, p175
108. Dubourdieu's Statistical Survey
109. Pat McBride
110. Dickie Duffin
111. Paddy Donnelly (deceased) Ballycastle
112. Hugh Duncan (deceased) Ballycastle
113. McCahan's Local Histories
114. Greer, Hamilton & Gailey, Ballymoney
115. Dickie Duffin
116. Alex McKay (deceased)
117. Jamie Davidson
118. The Rise and Decline of The Ballycastle Coalfield and Associated Industries, 1720 – 1840
119. Griffith Valuation, p57
120. Dickie Duffin
121. Griffith Valuation, pp 64,79,51,52
122. John McAuley, Manchester
123. Geology of North Antrim, p6. McCahan
124. Dickie Duffin
124. Geology of North Antrim, p11. McCahan
126. Dickie Duffin, John McConnell Ballycastle and John Hill, Ballycastle
127. Griffith Valuation, pp 55, 79
128. Glynns Vol 21, p.70
129. Dickie Duffin, who played cards here
130. Newspaper cutting in McCahan's scrap book
131. Lily Collins (deceased)
132. John McAuley, Manchester
133. Dickie Duffin
134. Dan Duncan
135. John McAuley and Jamie Davidson
136. Griffith Valuation, pp 55, 74
137. Danny McGill, Ballinlea
138. Dickie Duffin
139. Andy McLernon (deceased), Ballycastle

140. Cornelius Boyle and John McAuley
141. Mairead Fisher, Novally
142. Grand Jury Presentation Book for County Antrim, Summer Assizes, 1849, pp 170, 171
143. Dickie Duffin
144. Jamie Davidson
145. Pat McMullan (deceased)
146. Griffith Valuation, pp 54, 57, 58
147. Glynns Vol 21, pp 68, 75
148. Glynns Vol 1, p.11
149. Lesley Brook, Dunedin, New Zealand (personal communication)
150. Griffith Valuation pp 51, 55, 56
151. Jamie Davidson
152. Dickie Duffin
153. John McAuley
154. Dan Duncan
155. Dickie Duffin
156. Glynns Vol 2, p.19
157. The Irish Language in Rathlin Island, Co. Antrim, p. 175. Nils M. Holmer, Royal Irish Academy, Dublin, 1942.
158. Diocese of Down & Connor Vol 4, pp 479, 480, by Rev. James O'Laverty P.P., M.R.I.A. 1982 reprint by Davidson Books, Spa, Ballynahinch, Co. Down
159. Glynns Vol 17, p.34 (Danny McGill article), and the notes of the late Anthony McKinley
160. John McAuley

Chapter Two – North Star Mine to Torr

"All the old mines around the shore have been re-opened and large quantities of coal are being produced. The largest output is from the Griffen Mine which is worked by night and day. The North Star Mine is yielding a considerable quantity and pumping machinery is being installed at the White Mine. The slack is carted to Ballyvoy where there are new brick kilns in operation. The new managing director is Mr. Allerton, McNeill is the general manager and Mr. Heckie, the underground manager.

The older inhabitants say that the place is now beginning to look similar to what it appeared years ago, when Messrs. Merry and Cunningham, or Gordon and McDonald were the proprietors." This was the optimistic report of a local newspaper in February, 1908,[1] but for the White Mine, Griffin and the North Star', it was another false dawn.

North Star Mine, 1987

The mine entrance, now sealed, is almost directly opposite the North Star Dyke, hence the name. A Mr. MacIldowney (McGildowny) is said to have worked coal in this area about 1690.[2] But the North Star is not included among those mines which were recorded as being worked in the 1720's. Hugh Boyd (d1765) opened new mines at the Pans, the White Mine and Tornaroan some time after he gained control of the collieries, (the North Star is in Tornaroan townland). Thus the sandstone entrance which we know today may date from the Boyd period. Boyd drove his miners further and to a greater depth than previously had been the case.[3] Wm Hamilton visited the area in 1784, and he recorded the amazing discovery made at the North Star' c1770. Miners had come upon an ancient passage blocked with debris, and had excavated a hole large enough for two boys to squeeze through. Although furnished with candles, the boys were soon lost when they began exploring the maze of galleries and passages which lay beyond. The miners, alarmed at the non-return of the boys, began clearing away the debris, in order to effect a rescue. But it was not until the following day when the miners heard tapping that they managed to locate and rescue the pair. The experience did not deter James McKiernan and William McNeal, as both boys later became miners.

After the rescue the miners explored the area and discovered 36 chambers complete with supporting pillars at the correct intervals to support the roof. Strewn around were tools and baskets, but the latter disintegrated when touched. As there was no tradition of the mine having been worked earlier, Hamilton concluded that the workings had occurred some five centuries previously. This was based on the fact that particles of coal had been discovered in the lime mortar of Bruce's Castle, Rathlin. As there are no coal deposits on the island, Hamilton deduced that the source of these coal particles must have been Ballycastle.[4] On Williamson's 1787 map, the North Star' is marked as No 10, with the coal at 256 yards.

The Rev William Bisset visited the collieries on 18th August 1799, as he was fascinated by Hamilton's account, and wished to speak to the miners. They confirmed everything that Hamilton had stated, adding that they had found the stones on which the tools were sharpened, the "Hassocs" on which the men sat, and some of the "Instruments" used.[5] Another account of ancient workings comes from Andy McLernon, who worked to Jamie Delargy carting coal from Goldnamuck mine in the 1940's. He recalled seeing old creels which crumbled to dust when touched. They were made from hazel, were semi-circular in shape, with a flat side which had leather straps.

The old mines were low in height; this necessitated the creel being strapped to the collier's back as he haunched his way towards the entrance. There may have been lidded creels used in the areas where the miners were forced to crawl. A number of alcoves or chambers were also discovered where the miners rested on crudely shaped stone seats.[6] The North Star Mine in the 1800's saw a century of bouts of feverish activity, followed by periods of closure. Griffith does not record the North Star' nor any Tornaroan mine in operation in 1860/1.

Lagglass

The 19th century saw a steady stream of visitors to the collieries. Many of these tourists were quick to voice their opinions of how wretched the mines were, and that the miners were an indolent lot. Few of the critics actually entered a mine, never mind conduct a serious exploration. They gave various reasons for not venturing in to the bowels of the earth, there was the foul air, the lack of ventilation and flooded pits. But the miners had to contend with all of this daily, plus the ever present danger of serious injury or death from rock falls. Some mines were infested with rats and there was always the risk of a premature explosion.

At the base of a cliff ESE of the North Star' is an airshaft to the mine. Presently the entrance is constricted due to a rock fall and one has to crawl to gain admittance. Beyond this obstacle the shaft is said to be quite spacious. John Hill and Donald Campbell spent an entire day in the mine and airshaft carrying out exploratory work on behalf of Lord Antrim. A feature here was that the coal was filled through chutes into bogies below. In a flooded section of the mine they discovered an abandoned bogie, where it remains to this day. The coal was taken out through both airshaft and mine. At Ballyreagh there is another airshaft which is said to have been a channel to the North Star'.[7] The North Star' was last worked in the early

1950's. Waste material from the mine was taken out in bogies to a roadside turn table, then tipped to the shore below.[8]

The sandstone arch of the North Star Mine has a grill on the entrance sealing its fate for all time. There were a number of mines in this area, but their history has vanished with the previous generation. Bob Butler, Ballyvoy, worked in a small mine above the North Star' in 1952, with his brother Alex and Dan McKiernan.[9]

Approximately halfway between the North Star Dyke and Marconi's Cottage[10] there was the West Mine, worked in the 1720's. Its position is above the road but below the old cart track which leads up to Tornaroan. The 1787 map records the West Mine old level, with coal at 600 yards.[11] On the first O.S. map surveyed in 1832, the West Mine Colliery is recorded, but the mine may not have been operating.

Today there is no trace of the West Mine, and even the name is obsolete. The cart track to Tornaroan, long since abandoned, is marked by sections of a sandstone wall. Two and a half centuries ago this must have been a bustling place used by farmers, miners, kelp-burners, fishermen, quarrymen and others. Lagmore mine was worked as early as 1724[12] but appears to have been abandoned after a brief period. Nearby is Lagglass, the site of another early mine, both are on Boyle's farm, above "Marconi's Cottage". Both placenames are in current use, the former means 'large hollow', and the latter means 'green hollow'. But today Laglass is the larger of the two indicating the unstable nature of the terrain with landslides changing the face of the landscape. With Lagglass, the raw gap left behind must have been quickly covered by fresh vegetation.

One such landslide which occurred many years ago claimed two lives. A couple lived in a house almost opposite "Marconi's Cottage" and one night their house was swept away by a landslide. Their bodies were never found, although the carcass of a pig was washed up. The names of the couple have long been forgotten. There was said to have been a smithy here and about World War Two a pair of blacksmith's tongs were discovered, which gave weight to the oral tradition. The tongs have since been lost.[13]

Marconi's Cottage, 1987

This was another area where locals went to hoke coal. Dickie Duffin recalled the day that he and two other men entered an old mine. They had filled a few bags of coal when suddenly a stone fell from the roof of the mine. The men decided that it was best to get out, and had just done so when the mine caved in. They had observed the warning, acted upon it, and lived to tell the tale. The site of this mine has remained buried ever since.[14]

Below Laglass there is a rock face inscribed with the dates 1813, 1951 and there is also a double "H" carved. This reminds me of the TV aerial that I discovered at the base of a cliff, after a storm some years ago.! Beyond the North Star Mine the road swells out to form a little carpark. There was said to have been a mine here below the road known as the Arch Mine, where the coal was drawn out by horses.[15] Apart from the oral tradition of this one source, there is no corroborating evidence of a mine at this location.

Below the carpark is a buttress wall of well cut sandstone blocks, and a broad flight of steps (now built up) led down to Tornaroan Port.[16] The carparking area has been identified by Danny McGill as the site of the West Mine Saltpans which appear to date from the 1720's.[17]

Stone inscribed 1817 at "Marconi's Cottage"

"Marconi's Cottage" was formerly known as the Coalyard Cottage,[18] the date of its construction, 1817, is inscribed on the sandstone wall. The old residents also knew the cottage as "Call-the-Coals", as it had been built as a coalyard, and the man in charge used to call out the weight of the coal.[19] Jack McAllister and Johnny Kerrigan were two men who worked here, residing in the cottage, at different periods. The latter gathered and burned kelp. Other residents of the cottage include the Manning and McAuley families.[20]

A number of myths have grown up around the old coalyard and its dwelling house. Some tourist brochures have stated that Guglielmo Marconi resided here for a time, and one even stated that he had built the structure! These claims are bogus as Marconi's accommodation for his four nights in Ballycastle was the Antrim Arms Hotel. A brass plaque in the hotel's lounge commemorating the link with Marconi was unveiled by his daughter, Princess Elettra Gionvanelli in July 1998. Blue Circle plaques have been erected at two other locations associated with Marconi's experiments, 45 North Street, Ballycastle, and at the East Light, Rathlin.

There was once a plaque at the front of Marconi's Cottage but as its inscription was erroneous, the plaque was removed. Ever since, a fierce debate has raged over the precise link between Marconi and the cottage. One school of thought is that the first radio signals from Rathlin were received by Marconi's assistant in the Coalyard in 1898. This view was held by the late David Dillon who had researched the subject over a number of decades. The second theory is that the Marconi Company used the cottage when they returned to Ballycastle in 1905, and that the name dates from then.[21] Another theory is that W.H. Preece used the cottage in connection with his wireless telephony and telegraphy signals (Morse Code) experimentation in 1899.[22] With these three separate experiments all carried out within a decade in the one geographical area it is not surprising that such ambiguity exists over the name.

These historic events have not been forgotten and have been commemorated in a number of ways. Marconi Park and Kemp Park (named after Marconi's assistant) are sited near Ballycastle Chapel, which itself had been used in the 1898 experiments. Cross and Passion College, Moyle Road, has a Marconi Science Department which was officially opened by Princess Elettra in July, 1998. The Ballycastle based Marconi Radio Group MIO MRG has a membership of amateur radio enthusiasts drawn from throughout North Antrim and the Coleraine areas. Every August they hold a Marconi Festival, with radio transmissions throughout the day. The Marine Hotel has its Marconi Bar and there was a Marconi Memorial on the Quay Hill.

Marconi's achievements have inspired English composer Robert Jarvis to write a piece of music entitled, "Sparks and Waves".[23] Medhbh McGuckian has produced a book of poetry, entitled "Marconi's Cottage" and Corner Stone Crafts, Ballycastle, produced commemorative toasters to mark the centenary. Edward Edwin Glanville, Marconi's engineer, was born in Dublin, 1873, and had studied wireless technology under Professor Fitzgerald at Trinity College, Dublin. Glanville's premature death in a cliff fall in Rathlin, 21st August 1898, led to his important role in the experiments being largely overlooked. A new book by Professor Michael Sexton, University College Cork, has helped to redress this imbalance.

On Rathlin a new plaque was unveiled in 2005 which includes Glanville's involvement in the experiments, previously his name had been omitted. Another Dublin link to the 1898 experiments was the financial support given by Jamesons Distillery. This was due to the fact that Anne Jameson married Giuseppe Marconi in 1864, and they became the parents of Guglielmo.[24]

The distillery celebrated the centenary in 1998 with the release of a limited edition of Jameson Special Reserve Irish Whiskey. But the Technological Museum in Ballycastle to mark the achievements of Marconi, Kemp and Glanville has yet to be realized. Perhaps by the time of the 150th anniversary the dream will have come to fruition.

Opposite Marconi's Cottage are a number of cultivation ridges in poor soil, evidence of subsidence farming. At the rear of the cottage are a line of square post holes from a long forgotten pier. A few yards east of the boundary fence is a settling pan and channel where salt was extracted from seawater.[25] Beyond lies Murry's Port, where a miner of that name kept a boat for fishing and also probably for boating coal.[26] The 1734 Census does not record the name in the area, but there was a John and Cathy Murray here by the 1820's. The 1669 Hearth Money Rolls record Pat O'Murry at Ballinlea, Dermot O'Murry at Moyarget and Jer Boy McMurry at Cross (Fair Head).[27] Henry Murry in 1860 resided at Drumaridley where he held 11 acres, two roads and 20 perches.[28] While the Murrys may be of Irish or Scots origin, many of those in N. Antrim will be of the O'Murry clan of the Glens. The name signifies grandson of the mariner.[29]

At Murry's Port there is an ancient mine which had by the 18th century vanished from view, after a landslide. A few years ago another landslide revealed an arched sandstone entrance, about High Water Level. The location is approximately two thirds of the way from Marconi's Cottage to the Iron Stage. A steady trickle of water pours out of the mine entrance and nearby is a line of massive boulders. They are the base of the roadway which ran to Carrickmore, and from there a track continued to Portnaloub. The roadway in this section has largely disappeared. This area was worked in the 1720's, and is recorded on the 1787 map as Upper Muck Level, and Low Muck Shaft.[30]

A number of mines were worked over the centuries at Goldnamuck, but much of the evidence has been obscured by landslides. During the 1926 General Strike no coal was imported into Ireland for six months, and this gave a fresh impetus to the Ballycastle mines. The following extract is culled from Robert McCahan's scrapbook. About July, three miners named Carr, Rankin and Herrigan who had worked in Scotland began working Goldnamuck. They were soon followed by Robert Nasmith from Lanarkshire. He was joined by compatriot named Muir and his son at his pit, where they struck a seam of Main Coal.[31] Another miner who worked here in 1926 was Denis Delargy.[32]

James Delargy worked Goldnamuck in 1947-8, he "robbed" the pillars in the Main Coal, and used the coal for lime-burning. The lorry driver was Kearney, who later became a butcher in Waterfoot.[33]

Mick McAuley worked as a miner at Goldnamuck during the Big Snow of 1947. His family recall one particularly bad evening when they were concerned for his welfare, but he managed to get home safely. Davey Duffin, Ballycastle, who worked to Paddy Dallat, was a lorry driver who drew the coal from Goldnamuck for a period.

Goldnamuck had a sandstone entrance, and the chisel marks of the dressed stone are clearly recalled. The coal was hauled out by winch, then tipped down a chute to a waiting lorry. An airway in the mine led up to the top of the cliff. This was not only a source of fresh air but it was also used as a short cut by a number of men on their way to and from work.[34] Beyond Goldnamuck are the remains of McGildowny's Pier, or Iron Stage as it is often called. The landward section, constructed of locally hewn sandstone, back-filled with earth and rubble, stood approximately 16 feet high.

Remains of the Iron Stage, from Goldnamuck

The Ballyvoy Pier as it is officially known was built by Merry & Cunningham, a Scottish firm about 1860.[35] William Pinkerton was a mason who worked on the construction of the pier. He died at Bath Lodge, 26th May 1900, and was buried in Culfeightrin.[36] The outward portion of the pier consisted of stanchions which ran to the end of the line of rocks where there was deep water. Bogies were square wagons which ran on rails, down to the pier head. Here the coal (and iron ore on occasions) was tipped down a chute, and into the hold of a waiting coalboat. The bogies appear to have been in operation until about the commencement of World War One. When not in use, local children were quick to use the bogies as new mechanical toys.

This was a period when few adults had even travelled in a motor vehicle and a baby's toy was a home made rattle. This consisted of a small square wooden box with a stone sealed inside.[37]

Iron Stage, 2003

During World War Two a number of Iron Stage stanchions were removed, along with many Ballycastle railings, in the War effort. For some reason a few stanchions were not scrapped, and were left in situ.[38] One by one, they fell, their mangled remains yet lie entangled amongst the rocks. The last surviving stanchion succumbed to the Winter Storms of 1987-8. The pier's stonework remained intact until the 1970's when the sea made a breach, leaching out the earth and rubble in-fill. This occurred on the West wall, and after some time the sandstone blocks began to collapse. At first this was a slow process, but increased momentum in recent years has removed half the pier. A number of blocks contained an area the size of a brick, neatly cut out. These blocks which were on the same level showed the position of the scaffolding timbers.

There is evidence in the form of a few rotting timbers projecting from the interior breast wall that scaffolding had been used here also. Sandstone from the Iron Stage was used to repair the Margy Bridge, damaged when a lorry crashed into the parapet. Four Antrim County Council employees were sent to remove 18 blocks from the Iron Stage. First the men had to cut out each individual stone, then haul it up the grassy slope to the old colliery roadway. Here the blocks were placed in a wheelbarrow and wheeled all the way to "Marconi's Cottage", where a lorry awaited them. After all the men's hard work on a difficult job, there was a surplus of stone when the bridge repairs were completed. This resulted in a string of expletives![39] Jack McDuff, a fireman on the Ballycastle Narrow Gauge for over 25 years was also a skilled craftsman. He obtained timber from the Iron Stage, from which he constructed the stairs of his new Rathlin Road house.

The pier also provided the wood from which Jack made a dresser for the late Jamie Campbell, Ballycastle. This dresser is now in the possession of Jamie's son, George. Jack McDuff was a fine fiddler who is said to have composed a number of tunes.[40] A local man recalls as a boy being given toys by Jack, which he had personally made. Jack, who died in September 1954, aged 68, is buried in St. Patrick and St. Brigid's, Ballycastle.[41] On a flat rock a few yards East of the Iron Stage are a number of square post holes, evidence of an earlier pier. Coal from the adjacent mines was sent out from here, hence the spot is known as Colliery Port.

Iron Stage, East flank

The name is almost obsolete now, as local fishermen ceased using this port in the 1960's. Even the winch used to haul up the boats is now gone.

Among the last to fish from the Colliery Port were P.J. McCambridge, Ballynaglogh, Denis Kerr, miner, and the Huggins brothers. The latter formerly kept their boat at Carrickmore, Denis Kerr's boat was an old tarred one known as The Coffin. It is believed to have been bought from "Devil" Archie Rodgers, Templastragh.[42] Joe McAllister, son of Jack, kept a boat here before World War Two.[43] The Clarkes of Murlough had a boat called "Una" which they kept here in the mid 1950's.[44] Hector McLean had a boat which was built locally at Blackpark. One afternoon while tied up at Colliery Port, it was lost in a storm.[45]

Kelp was also collected, dried and burned here, one of the pits is hidden by bracken in the hollow below the roadway. Local tradition is that the burned kelp was shipped out from the Iron Stage.[46] The names of only a few of the kelp burners are recalled today, Jamie and Johnny Kerrigan and Paddy Glenfield, Ballyvoy. The latter was a Loughguile man, his family have now died out locally.[47] A few yards beyond the kelp pit is a portion of a sandstone wall on a steep slope. The location of this wall is puzzling as it does not appear to have any obvious purpose. The wall ended on a large boulder which served as its foundation. This was a very unstable base, as high tides would have rocked the boulder, thus weakening the structure.

Iron Stage, last stanchion, 1987

In the early 1800's there were three buildings between the Iron Stage and the sloping wall. The largest one was a coalyard, oblong in shape and situated along the roadway. Coal from the Goldnamuck and Pollard mines was stored here until it could be shipped out. The two smaller buildings were on a lower level, one may have been a boathouse, the other a kelp store or a forge. Today there is no trace of the buildings, as the stone was removed to be used elsewhere. Even the foundations of the buildings have been obliterated by landslides.

Pollard Colliery extends from the Iron Stage to a basalt dyke approximately 200 yards eastwards. The name, from the Gaelic Poll Ard, means high pit as the Main Coal seam occurs higher here that at nearby Goldnamuck. An 1829 report states of Pollard that it was one of the six mines worked to a very considerable extent by 1724.[47] The 1787 map records No 13, Polard Level, 546 yards in, and Polard shaft, 472 yards to the coal.[48] By the early 19th century at least three mines had been opened at Pollard. One is easily found today near the summit of the cliff, its position pinpointed by a spoil heap not yet covered by vegetation.

Remains of boundary wall, Colliery Port

Behind this mine is a grassy hollow, caused by subsidence due to mining operations. The evidence is at the base of the hollow where a section of the mine has been exposed. A short distance East, hidden around a corner is a second mine. Here the seam of coal outcrops on the cliff face just above a ledge. This may be the original Pollard mine as it was an obvious location for the early miners to explore.

At the base of this cliff is a third mine, its entrance sealed with earth, creating the perfect camouflage. Inscribed on the adjacent rock face is a name, now faint and almost illegible due to weathering. The personal name is almost certainly Johnny, and the surname appears to be Cushnahan. A roadway connected this mine with two at a higher level, all trace of the route has now disappeared, buried under the scree. Rising above the cliff is the hill of Crockateemore, pronounced Crooketymore by an older generation.[49] The name translates as hill of the big house. This was said to have been a large house, used as a colliery office, which had disappeared by the 1850's.[50] there are the remains of two cairns here and there was a sandstone quarry in operation in the 19th century.

At Pollard there is a second quarry on the cliff face, marked by a broad ledge and an area of worked stone. This proves that the sandstone was dressed in situ before it was cut and shaped into blocks. There were a number of other sandstone quarries worked in the parish during the 18th and 19th centuries. Their locations were at Ballyreagh, Ballynagard, Tornaroan and Broughanlea where there were two sandstone quarries. One was at the Pans Rocks, and the second was at the entrance to the White Mine, now a camping site.[51]

The latter, worked by Hugh Boyd in the 1730's, became the subject of a legal dispute with Lord Antrim about 1740-1.[52] The 1720 lease by the McGwires of Ballyreagh Quarry included the right to remove stone limestone and clay for brick-making.[53] Ballynagard sandstone quarry was in a field to the rear of McBride's bungalow, 15 Ballynagard Road. This quarry has long since been filled in, and only the name, Quarry Field, survives.[54] Stone from here was used in the construction of Carey Chapel in the early 1800's.[55]

By the time of Griffith's Valuation however the quarry had closed. Griffith records a sandstone quarry at Ballyvoy, and another at Tornaroan, both leased by John Wilkinson off John McGildowny, Clare Park.[56] This is obviously the same John Wilkinson who in 1852 possessed the "Freestone Quarries at Ballycastle Colliery."[57] The Wilkinsons, known locally as McQuilkin, moved to the Bushmills area many years ago. Few names of those who worked in the sandstone quarries are known;
Charles McAlister, Drumadoon, stonecutter, 1864
John Darragh, Ballycastle, stonecutter,1868
Dan Darragh, Ballycastle, stonecutter, 1869

Dyke which separates Pollard and Griffin collieries

A trade directory records a James Hill working the sandstone quarries in 1908. Local sandstone has been used in many of Ballycastle's older buildings, and elsewhere in properties such as Mussenden Temple and Downhill Castle.[58] The freestone in the arcade and on the inside of the windows of St. Patrick's Parish Church, Coleraine, came from Ballycastle. The stone is described as of a peculiar light tint, and the work was carried out in 1883/4.[59] Sandstone was once used extensively in the construction industry, and not only as building stone. More specialized uses included bollards, columns, coping stones, corbels, door steps, floor tiles, finials, keystones (in arches), lintels, quoins, ridge tiles and window sills. Ecclesiastical uses included architraves, baptismal fonts, crosses, headstones and plaques. Other miscellaneous products included caps for wells, garden rollers, grindstones, mill stones, sharpening stones (scythe stones), standing stones and troughs.

Sandstone standing stones are not common, but there is one at Aghaleck, Glenshesk. Spindle-whorls for spinning, made from sandstone, were in use in Ireland up to the 17th century.[60] Pugmills used to crush clay in brickworks, were once made of sandstone.[61] The above list is incomplete, and more research is needed to determine if local sandstone was used in all the examples quoted.

Adjacent to Pollard is Griffin Colliery, the two are divided by a basalt dyke, which juts out into the sea approximately 28 yards. Griffin was one of the six mines recorded as having been worked to a very considerable extent by 1724.[62]

Coalyard site at Griffin

74

This was undoubtedly the most difficult colliery to work, given the cliffs and their scree covered slopes. The miners pronounced the place as Grief-in,[63] which may be an anglicisation of Gairbhín meaning "rough place".[64] By the 1830's there were four mines in operation here, one of which was above the roadway, in Ballyvoy townland. This mine has long since disappeared from view, but its approximate position is indicated by a spoil heap, raw and fresh after a recent landslide. The remaining three mines are situated in Ballyreagh Lower townland and they are over halfway up the cliff, while the fourth is below the roadway. The latter is in a swampy hollow adjacent to the ruins of a small building which despite its small size may have been a clerk's office.

A few yards West was a mine, its entrance is now sealed, but from which there is seepage of iron ore scum. An iron bar protruding from a boulder on the store indicates that a winch was used to draw the coal from this mine. There is another example of a winch being used for this purpose at Carrickmore.

Remains of a building at Griffin

A roughly constructed boulder wall here has been back filled to create a level area, possibly as an unenclosed coalyard. From here a roadway extended East at High Water Level, towards a wooden pier known as Gobb Oul Stage. This lower roadway is now almost totally obliterated, only two short sections are to be seen, and then only with some difficulty. Another roadway ran at an angle up the lower slopes of the cliff, until blocked by the scree. This roadway which has survived is clearly visible from the fence which forms the boundary between Ballyvoy and Ballyreagh townlands.

Above the scree is the remains of a small basalt building which may well have been a store. In the early 1800's there were two mines above the building, one to the East and the other to the West. Near the latter at the base of a sheer rock is a water-filled mine entrance above which is a barely legible date, 1884. On a higher level is an old spoil heap, partially covered by heather, but there is no trace of the mine. Somewhere in this area in 1817 was a mine known as the Fox's Den. In that year, Robert O'Mullan, Patrick McGawley and Patrick Dixon were rewarded a contract to repair a section between Ballyvoy bridge and the Fox's Den.[65]

The Belfast Coal and Iron Limited, 60 Ann Street, Belfast, with an address at South Hill, Quay Road, Ballycastle, worked a number of mines in 1906. On 21st December 1906 the company announced an increase in the price of their coal to eleven shillings a ton (55p). This was stated to be due to the costs of opening a new level in the Griffin mine, which was worked 24 hours a day. Griffin was the most productive mine of the company's six mines and in February, 1908, their coal was selling at £1 per ton. Unscreened coal sold at 19 shillings (95p) per ton, but by July 1908, all production ceased.[66]

Heckie, Aiton and Kerr reopened the Griffin mine in May, 1917. They sold the coal delivered to Ballycastle at 35 shillings (£1.75) per ton. A year later the coal was selling at 41 shillings (£2.05) per ton. By April 1919, Griffin had closed.[67] There is no record of the mine ever having been worked again. Dickie Duffin recalled the mine in operation. About 10 men worked here, three of them from "over the mountain". One of the latter was a McBride, who may have been a Cushendall man. Willie Duffin, Dickie's uncle, lived at Mill Street, Ballycastle, and worked at Griffin and later at Portnaloub. Willie also worked in the Scottish mines, and then emigrated with his family to America, settling in Buffalo. A son, Paddy, returned home[68] and died in Ballycastle in the 1990's.

Archie Brown & John Collins, Broughmore

John Collins was orphaned at an early age, and was reared by the Browns at Broughmore in Glenshesk. Despite his farming background, John became a miner, working at Carrickmore and later at Griffin where he was a foreman. John lived in New Row, a little street off Castle Street which was often referred to as Scarlett's Yard. The "yard" was demolished almost 40 years ago, and today the site forms part of the Castle Street carpark. John and his wife Mary in 1926 emigrated to Canada, his brother Paddy went to sea and little is known of him.[69]

Jamie Gallagher, a native of Creeslough, Donegal, is recalled by Joe Lyden and Dickie Duffin, working in Griffin. Bob Stewart was a local miner who was killed at Griffin. He had been checking the roof of the mine, probing with a crow bar, when suddenly there was a collapse. A Loughguile miner called Winters is said to have been killed at Griffin, but nothing else is known of this incident.[71]

The massive boulder, adorned with names and initials, which blocks the roadway at Griffin, is known as the Standin' Rock.[72] Along the shore there is a rock called the Saddle, which it resembles, but only at high water. This was a popular spot from which to fish, but dangerous as one had to jump to reach it. A Ballyvoy man named Lynn who went to fish here slipped, fell in and drowned, his body was later recovered at Carrickmore.

Dickie Duffin and Johnny Henry were two Ballycastle men who often fished on the Saddle.[73] Nearby is Monroe Rock where a man named Monroe drowned while fishing, about the end of World War One. He was not a local.[74] In Ballyreagh Lower there is a flattish outcrop of rock, which was the site of a wooden pier. The Griffin and Gobb coal was sent out from this pier, which the locals called the Gobb Oul Stage.

The old-timers considered this a great location to fish glashan, but it was also dangerous. A deep channel cuts through the rock, dividing it into two sections, forcing one to jump across, which is particularly risky at high tide.[75] Jamie Davidson, Drumnakeel, often fished here. He recalled going down in the month of October about an hour before dusk. This was considered the best time for fishing. Boiled potatoes were broken up and thrown into the water to feed the glashan and lythe. On occasions a fire was lit, and limpets were cooked as bait, and white hair from a goat was also used to lure the glashan.

Fair Head from Griffin

Once when Jamie was short of bait he used a bit of tangle, and caught a few fish. It was said of glashan that "they would take anything." At Gobb the fish when caught were kept in a round hole in the rock until the fishermen were leaving. Bob Lynn and the Huggins brothers of Ballyvoy, Paddy McIlroy, Lisnacalliagh, and John McGill, Malladeevan, were a few who fished at Gobb.[76] The fishermen were recalled standing with their legs wide apart, and they had their bamboo rods wedged into rock crevices. This was done in order to brace themselves against the incoming waves.[77]

Jeanie McNeill's cottage, Coolanlough

Another man who fished at Gobb was Jamie McKiernan's grandfather, but he preferred a rock known as Louby.[78] John McCrank of Coolanlough was a farmer who got into difficulties while bathing at Gobb and drowned.[79] A boat was discovered washed up on the shore, near the site of the pier. There were a number of badly decomposed bodies onboard, and due to the risk of fever it was decided to bury the bodies on the spot. Between high water mark and the roadway is a level area and this was chosen as the site for the grave.

The bodies of the sailors (thought to have been three) were placed on old boards which were lying about, and carried up to the grave. The ground was consecrated by the parish priest of Carey and the local minister, and they also held a service. The gravediggers were local men who were paid to carry out the risky and unpleasant task. The boat lay where it was beached until it rotted away; no one went near it, such was the fear of fever. In a short space of time the spot became known as the Sailor's Grave.[80]

Some time later there was a landslide and a rock ended upright at the head of the grave. The stone had a rounded top and from a distance, resembled a headstone.[81]

Gobb is an area of cliffs, extending from Griffin to Freestone Point, and the name is from the Gaelic Gob, meaning a snout or beak like point. Richard Griffith states that Gobb was one of the six mines that were worked to a very considerable extent as early as 1724. This was evident from the plan and section of the colliery, Plate No 4 made

Sailors Grave, near Griffin

in that year. Griffith states that he was grateful to Mr. McNeil of Ballycastle for a copy of the plan, Plate No 4. Samuel Wright (1790-1847) did a scientific tour of County Antrim in 1806. He remarks that the Gobb colliery seems that which is most worked at present – in most of the mines is a good deal of water and the men are frequently obligated to break off in consequence for want of ventilation – but I strongly suspect it much owing to want of industry, they appear to be an indolent race of people. Previously Wright states that the "Galleries" (mines) were in such a state that he dare not enter them![83]

Another visitor, Berger, is much more sympathetic when speaking of Gobb in 1813. He states that the mines suffered so much from foul air that they could not stay more than 8 hours out of 24 in the mine. This is despite the fact that Gobb appears to have been relatively well supplied with air. An 1817 plan shows a number of such features, Cape Horn, Paugh's Arch, Sandy Dyke Airway and one described as Old Airway.

A number of old tram roads are shown, as in Mr. Magawley's Tramway.[84] Gobb was being worked by Mr. McNeil, agent to the Boyd Estate in the 1820's. Previously Mr. Boyd had worked the coal but he was unable to keep the mine from being flooded.[85]

The Parliamentary Gazetteer, Vol. 1, 1846 mentions "the curious abandoned coal-mines" of Culfeightrin Parish. There is no reference to Gobb ever having been worked again, and of the Gobb Grand Level, there is now not the slightest trace. A roadway runs at an angle, then ends abruptly approximately half way up the cliff, under the scree. This roadway and the adjacent spoil heap relate to another mine which has vanished from view. A short distance past the site of the Gobb mines is an oblong area cut in the sandstone on the foreshore. This has all the appearance of a swimming pool, but is in fact a settling pan, where salt was extracted from seawater. Dr Wm. Petty's Down Survey map of 1657 shows a saltpan on the boundary of Ballyreagh and Ballyvoy. Although the settling pan is just East of the Ballyvoy boundary at Griffin, this is reasonably close for such an early map.

The 1720 lease of the collieries to the McGwires included saltpans at Ballyreagh Upper and Lower.[86] Somewhere in this area was the Saltpans Dyke, as Samuel Wright refers to it during his tour in 1806.[87] Coneybeare and Buckland also mention the dyke[88] but the placename has long been obsolete.

Past the settling pan the roadway peters out, a rough track skirts the base of Freestone Point before reaching the level floor of Carrickmore. Along the high part of the track is a graffiti covered rock and below is a mysterious cave known only to a few. The cave is nameless, difficult to locate and has no tradition of smuggling, nor fugitives having been concealed here. Yet both activities have occurred in the area. East of the cave is Portnagree, in Gaelic Port na Groigh (the gh is silent), meaning port of the horse drove.[89]

There is another Portnagree at Ballycastle, but at both places the place-name has declined, in direct relation to the slump in fishing. Portnagree is a short distance West of the stream which forms the boundary of Ballyreagh Upper townland. There is no record of mining having taken place here prior to the death of Hugh Boyd in 1765. Williamson's 1787 map[90] gives No 17 Portnagree level, 40 yards in and the relatively short distance hints that the mine had not been operating long.

By the mid 19th century another three mines had been opened, and in one mine both coal and iron ore was worked. The level area on both sides of the stream is formed of waste material, and the area became known as the Hearths. Iron working in the Fair Head region dates back centuries, as an excavation at Doonmore revealed. The report states that a bloom of Iron found in the workshop shows that the metal was melted on the site.[91] Griffith's Valuation records Sheppard, Berril and Company as having an Ironstone mine at Cross, leased off the Earl of Antrim, with offices leased off James Butler at Ballyreagh Upper.

Merry and Cunningham were a Scottish firm who worked the iron ore at Carrickmore about 1860. They used coal from the White Mine to calcine the ore, which was then shipped to Scotland for smelting. The company had a wooden jetty at Carrickmore, and from here two and occasionally three shipments were made each week. The two vessels engaged in this trade were both small steamers, the "Glengarnoch" and the "Jesse Brown". When Cunningham and Merry's lease ended the company transferred all their machinery from Carrickmore to their new operation at Bilboa in Spain. A smithy built at Carrickmore in 1856, was in ruins by about 1885, and today there is not a trace of the building.[92]

John McGildowny, Clare Park, also worked the iron ore for a period, and on his death in October, 1887, he was succeeded by his son Hugh. After the ore was calcined, the waste matter was left strewn around where it often ignited spontaneously, giving off gas and vapour. John Butler of Ballyreagh Lower in 1892 claimed compensation against Hugh McGildowny. Extraction of the ore appears to have ceased by the start of the Great War, and today there is little evidence that the industry ever existed. There are sandstone buttresses, walls and the remains of a bridge in the area of The Hearths. There are also various irons embedded in the three rock islands which are collectively known as Carrickmore.

Carrickmore

The leveled area on the summit of the rocks clearly shows the position of the wooden pier, at the end of which there was deep water. Below The Hearths is a small sandstone arch with its entrance choked with debris. A constant stream of water flows from the arch, but this is not a culvert. It is the Arched Mine in which both coal and iron ore was worked. The coal and iron ore was drawn out in bogies, operated by a pulley system. Part of the thin pulley frame remains, rusting away and battered by waves.[94]

Only a few of the names of those who worked at Carrickmore are known. Paddy McBride, grandfather of the late Pat McBride, Ballyreagh, was a miner at Carrickmore, who earned six pence per day. He was almost 90 when he died. Jamie Harrigan, grandfather of the late Steven Harrigan, Ballycastle, worked the ironstone at Carrickmore.[95] Patrick Mulligan who came from near Arklow was killed in a rock fall, 17th July, 1868, he was employed by Merry and Cunningham.[96] Another casualty was Glenravel man Hugh McKay who was killed in an accident in an ironstone mine.[97] Archibald Gray was Merry and Cunningham's Mine Manager in 1871.[98]

Mining continued intermittently at Carrickmore, up to the early 1920's. In November 1920 Raymond McConville with John Reid as his partner, began clearing out the old Carrickmore mine, on the face of the cliff. They encountered many blockages, but as soon as these were cleared, new rock falls occurred.

Finally in September, 1922, the two men abandoned the mine which was then worked by three of their former employees. William Duffin, James Gallagher and a miner named McIlroy were working a 22 inch seam of coal in November, 1922. They also removed the supporting pillars of coal, which were left to support the roof of the old mine. These stoups were between 5 and 10 yards square, and the output of the three miners was five tons per fortnight.

In January 1923, coal was sold at 35 shillings (£1.75) per ton, which included 10 shillings (50p) for transportation to Ballycastle. A better grade of Carrickmore coal was selling at £3 per ton in Ballycastle in January, 1921. The three miners were forced to abandon their tools and hutches when the mine in which they were working was flooded with water from a higher mine. A new mine was then opened by the men, and at approximately 560 yards they reached coal.

By February, 1923, Carrickmore was abandoned,[99] and The Hearths which had been a hive of industrial activity was now grazed by sheep. The old Ballycastle fishermen never fished on a Sunday, but took their families for picnics by boat to Ballintoy, Kenbane, Murlough and Carrickmore. The late Dickie Duffin recalled seeing five boats at Carrickmore on a Sunday afternoon. West of the waterfall was a spring which supplied the fresh water for making tea.[100] Another group which held picnics here were the pupils of The Row School. Every year on the day before the school closed for summer holidays the children were taken on their annual excursion to The Hearths.[101]

Carrickmore has had its share of tragedy over the years, with drownings and bodies cast upon the shore from afar. An undated cutting in the McCahan scrapbook gives one such example. A body washed ashore at Carrickmore was off the armed merchant cruiser, Viknor, which was sunk near Rathlin near six weeks ago. "Full naval and military honours were accorded at the burial in Bonamargy. Sergeant P. Brannigan, Royal Irish Constabulary; Company Commander Arthur Hunter and J.A. Byrne were in charge of a company of Ulster Volunteers. There was a company of National Volunteers under J.D. Coghlan, Francis Black, Rural District Council and E. Savage. J. Ainsworth, R. N. Divisional Officer, Coastguard, Ballycastle, also attended." HMS Viknor was lost on the night 13th January, 1915, somewhere between Tory Island and Irishtrahull.

HMS Racoon perished in a snowstorm on the morning of 9th January, 1918, somewhere off the North coast of Ireland. There were no survivors from either vessel,[102] and a number of the victims were interred at Ballintoy, Rathlin and Bonamargy. Four bodies, identified as members of the crew of HMS Viknor and eight from HMS Racoon are interred in the area of Bonamargy known as the Poor Ground.

F.HARVEY
ABLE SEAMAN, R.N. J/21488
HMS RACOON
9TH JANUARY 1918

E.F. WALTER
MECHANICIAN R.N. 282791
HMS RACOON
9TH JANUARY 1918

PO/7084 PRIVATE RMLI
J GRIFFIN
HMS VIKNOR
13TH JANUARY 1915

W.H. Mc KAY
STOKER 1ST CLASS, R.N. SS/117528
HMS RACOON
9TH JANUARY 1918 AGE 24

HIS MEMORY LONG WILL LIVE
ALONE IN ALL OUR HEARTS
TENNYSON

A further four headstones bear the following inscription:

A SAILOR
OF THE GREAT WAR
ROYAL NAVY
HMS VIKNOR
13TH JANUARY 1915

A single headstone bears the inscription:

A SAILOR
OF THE GREAT WAR
ROYAL NAVY
HMS RACOON
9TH JANUARY 1918
KNOWN UNTO GOD

Another World War One headstone inscribed:

A SAILOR
OF THE GREAT WAR
UNKNOWN STOKER
ROYAL NAVY
30TH JUNE 1917

A solid Celtic Cross erected by O'Connor, Ballycastle, and embellished
with a harp, shamrocks and Celtic inter-lacing in inscribed:

ERECTED
BY
THE PEOPLE OF BALLYCASTLE
TO THE MEMORY OF
WILLIAM FAULKNER, STOKER 1ST CLASS
WILLIAM H. Mc KAY, STOKER 1ST CLASS
E.F. WALTER, MECHANICIAN.
J. HARVEY, A.B.
JAMES GRIFFIN, PRIVATE R.M.L.I.
4 SEAMEN AND 1 STOKER UNIDENTIFIED
HMS VIKNOR
WHO GAVE THEIR LIVES IN DEFENCE OF THE EMPIRE
IN THE GREAT WAR, 1914-1918.
WHOSE BODIES WERE CAST ASHORE ON THIS COAST,
AND INTERRED HERE.

Some additional information of this period is revealed in the diary of Peter
Dallat, undertaker, Ballycastle.[103]
   "6 April 1915 Lieutenant Ballentine from Portsmouth washed
ashore at the Strand. Buried in Bonamargy. Lifted in five weeks." This
implies that he was re-interred in Portsmouth.

"30 May 1915 Lieutenant Cooper washed ashore at Ballintoy"
"23 October 1918 Gustave Peterson, Sweden, aged 22 years."

The late Dickie Duffin recalled going with "Wee" Pat Hill, a local carter, to Ballintoy where they collected two bodies. The coffined corpses were taken on the back of a horse drawn cart to Doherty's store on Bayview Road (now the Bay Restaurant). Here the bodies were washed and dressed by Arthur Morgan. This was followed by the funeral to Bonamargy, which was led by the Ballycastle pipe band playing slow airs.

The following headstones in Bonamargy relate to the Second World War;

5255135 PRIVATE
E.C. JORDAN
THE WORCESTERSHIRE REGT.
6TH OCTOBER 1942

CAPTAIN
J.R. TOWNSEND
ROYAL CANADIAN ARTILLERY
30TH APRIL 1941 AGE 38
BELOVED HUSBAND OF
MABEL CRICH
AND DEAR FATHER OF JOHN
PATRICIA, ROBERT AND RODERICK.

1563285 AIRCRAFTMAN 2ND CL.
J. M^{C}DONALD
ROYAL AIR FORCE
21ST JANUARY 1942 AGE 18.

DROWNED AT SEA
SADLY MISSED BY ALL.

TO
THE MEMORY
OF
WILLIAM FISKEN
CHIEF RADIO OFFICER
MERCHANT NAVY
LOST AT SEA
21ST JANUARY 1942
AGED 45 YEARS
DEAR HUSBAND OF
NAN WEIR
HOME IS THE SAILOR
HOME FROM SEA
ALSO HIS WIFE
NAN WEIR
DIED AT GLASGOW
10TH SEPTEMBER 1960
AGED 66 YEARS.

A SAILOR
OF THE
SECOND WORLD WAR
MERCHANT NAVY
BURIED 11TH AUGUST 1940
KNOWN UNTO GOD
(TWO HEADSTONES)

A SAILOR
OF THE
SECOND WORLD WAR
MERCHANT NAVY
BURIED 23RD JUNE 1940
(TWO HEADSTONES)

The Templemore, Derry bound from Ellesmere Port with a cargo of coal, developed a list off Fair Head. The vessel sank in Ballycastle Bay with a loss of two lives.[104] A cutting dated 12/10/1912 gives an account of the attempts made to refloat the coalboat. Wrecked off Ballycastle on the 6th inst, she is lying in 12 fathoms of water, 3/4 mile off Ballycastle pier, in a position highly dangerous to shipping, as the height of the steamer from keel to main trunk is 70 feet. The wreck was buoyed on Wednesday afternoon by Ballycastle Shipping Company Ltd. (Lloyd's Agents) with a black barrel buoy. The barque "Fecamp", owned by McClausland & Son was sunk by water ballast over the Templemore. In that position both vessels were lashed together. The salvage ship St. Anthony stood alongside with massive pumps fitted on her. The water is then pumped out of the barque, which then rises bringing with her the Templemore. Both are them towed into more shallow water where the operation is repeated.[105] This salvage attempt failed and the wreck of Templemore lies on the seabed a short distance from the Pans Rocks.

Another vessel which came to grief off Fair Head was the Ballycastle Shipping Company's "Glentow". Returning to her port with a cargo of coal, the Glentow hit an under water reef at Portnaloub, approximately half a mile East of Carrickmore. Within days the vessel broke up and her wreckage lies strewn about the area. Part of the boiler and other sections lie along the shore at Portnaloub. One of the men who were waiting to unload the coal that morning was Dick Duffin, and he related the story to his son Dickie. The vessel carried a crew of five, one of whom, Joe Wilson, drowned a few years later.[106] The Ballycastle man is commemorated by a headstone in Bonamargy. The inscription, now barely legible, reads:

In Remembrance
A TOKEN OF RESPECT
FROM THE
OFFICERS AND CREW
OF THE S.S. CONISTON
TO THE MEMORY OF
JOSEPH WILSON
WHO WAS ACCIDENTLY DROWNED
IN THE THAMES ON 6TH JUNE 1922.

The Ballycastle shipping company was registered in December 1911, with a capital of £10,000 in £1 shares, taking over the business carried on H. McGildowny and J. Moorhead under the same name. The two men became directors, and the latter, who resided at North Street, was General Secretary for a period. Mr. A.S. Collard, J.P. of Liverpool joined the board of the company later that month. Hugh McGildowny, J.P., Clare Park, erected a pier in 1891 on the isolated rock of Craignascarf. This pier, which became known as McGildowny's Pier, was extended in 1898, due to the increased volume of trade.

Mr. McGildowny was a naval architect and he planned to connect his pier by rail along the River Tow to the railway station. But this ambitious scheme never materialized, no doubt due to the numerous problems which it would have encountered. At the inauguration of the new pier in 1891, Mr. McGildowny was presented with an illuminated address on behalf of the people of Ballycastle. This item came up at a public auction in 1985, and was purchased by a local man who lived within sight of the pier. The Board of Trade granted a lease dated 10th August, 1908, to Hugh McGildowny of a strip of land adjacent to the pier. He began to build up what is now known as the Pier Yard to its present level.

This work led to a great number of complaints from local fishermen. Donald Black had set his lobster creels in the sound between "Wee Rathlin" and the shore, but this had been filled in. McGildowny had built walls on the foreshore, and heavy seas had washed some of these walls down, which prevented use of the Boatslip. The Board of Trade held an inquiry in to the allegations, and R.P. Woodside exhibited photos and maps of the area prior to the erection of the walls. A diver called Murray was called in to remove the stones and Neal Dallat removed about 100 tons of rubble. Despite all the objections, the Board of Trade granted McGildowny a second lease of land on 2nd August 1910.

McGildowny's Pier, Ballycastle, c1900.

In April 1910 John Coyle and Daniel Black requested the County Council to erect a winch at the Boatslip. A cargo of 156½ tons of Machrihanish coal was imported on the Glentow in August 1911. J.C. McGuigan carried out work at the Harbour in 1913.[107] This then is the background to McGildowny's development of a harbour at Ballycastle. Folk memory of the period recalls the blue and white funnel of the Glentow, which traded with Belfast, the Clyde, Maryport, Preston and the other ports. She carried a general cargo which included limestone from the Whiterocks, 200 yards distant, and basalt from the Stroanshesk Quarry, directly above the Whiterocks.

Disused winch at Carrickmore

There was also bauxite from Ballintoy, setts which came by barge from Kenbane, and kelp which came from a wider area. Near the Fisherman's Path (now closed) there was a Coastguards Watch-house, a weigh bridge and a smithy.[108] The limestone was drawn in bogies by ponies, which ensured that the blacksmith was kept busy. Each animal had three brass bells which jingled as they pulled the bogies along, thus sounding a warning of their approach. Despite this safety precaution, there were the inevitable accidents. The ponies were stabled at night in Clare Park, and one man who worked with the ponies was Paddy Hill, Drumawillan. Paddy's sons, John and Patsy, have proudly preserved the three bells of one pony which their father worked with.[109] There were upwards of 40 men employed at McGildowny in connection with the limestone quarry and the pier. The steam crane on the pier was worked by Joe McAllister.

Boiler plate of the S.S.Glentow, at Portnaloub

The Glentow, which replaced an earlier vessel, the Glenshesk, was usually moored on the East side of the pier. But in certain conditions she was moored to a concrete bollard on a rock on the West of the pier.[110] A brass plaque inscribed "Ballycastle Shipping Company" is said to be in possession of a Ballycastle resident, as is the bell of the Glentow. The "Druid", a steamer outward bound for Glasgow from Ballycastle with a cargo of flint, struck a rock at Fair Head and sprung a leak. She turned back and arrived safely at the pier about 4am. Here her cargo was discharged and arrangements made for a tug to tow the vessel to Glasgow.[111]

An American built sailing boat was found drifting in Rathlin Sound on Tuesday 2nd October, 1888. It was believed to have been a boat from Port Ellen, Islay, in which two youths had left the previous Saturday.[112] In St. James Church of Ireland, Ballycastle, there is a brass plaque commemorating another two drowning victims. The inscription reads:

In memory of
Cecil Sparrow Aged 20
And
Tom Hay Aged 19
Who were drowned off Fair Head
May 11th, 1985.
"In death they were not divided."
Erected by their friends in Ballycastle.

The men were colleagues in a Ballycastle bank and had bought a boat earlier that day in Cushendall. With a third man, named Moore, they set off to row back to Ballycastle. But off Fair Head a squall blew up, and as they were inexperienced with local conditions the men were soon in difficulties. The boat capsized throwing the men into the water. Moore, who was a non-swimmer, managed to cling on to the keel and survived. The bodies of the two who drowned were never recovered.[113]

Rev George Hill wrote of going to look at the remains of a large vessel which had been driven ashore during the previous night, about a mile eastward of Ballycastle Harbour. He states that the nine corpses "were piously laid side by side in the old cemetery of Bunn na mairge."[114]

Portnaloub

Returning to Carrickmore, this was not a very sheltered spot, but it was convenient for local farmers to keep their boats here. Recalled are, the Huggins, Ballyvoy, and McBrides, Ballyreagh, with boats at Carrickmore.[115] East of the stream is a well preserved kelp pit, a winch and more buttress walls. A flattish rock on the shore, called Carrickavadder, bears a number of post holes. This pier site, which gave Carrickmore its name, may well pre-date the Boyd era. From here a track continued for over a quarter of a mile to Portnaloub. The name translates as landing place of the loop, no doubt from some natural feature. Here, in the late 18th century, was the Nelson Colliery, but the name has never been explained, perhaps a person so named was involved in the colliery.

In 1793, boring was done in the blazing coal here, but no records were kept and the depth is not known. This is stated in an 1829 Report[116] by Richard Griffith (1784-1878). He surveyed the Leinster coalfields in 1808, and later he reported on the bogs of Ireland. In 1812 he became a Professor of Geology, and was appointed Minister of Mines. But he is best remembered for his "Primary Valuation of Tenements, 1848-1864", known to genealogists as Griffith's Valuation.[117] There is a reference in 1807 to the miners having to contend with "fauls", but within a few years the Nelson Colliery had closed. No coal appears to have been worked here until the early 20th century. The North Antrim Mining Syndicate sunk a shaft at Portnaloub and made an unsuccessful exploration for coal, as did Heckie, Aiton and Kerr.

John Reid discovered a seam of coal between $2\frac{1}{2}$ and $2\frac{3}{4}$ feet thick and had opened a mine here by 1921. That month the miners broke into the adit of an old mine which was arched and about nine feet wide. Owing to the danger of the mine entrance being flooded at high tide, Reid then sunk a shaft at some distance from the shore. The four foot seam of coal was described as very hard and very suitable for steam purposes. Above the coal was an eight foot seam of sandstone which provided a good roof. But as there was no demand locally for steam coal, Reid closed the mine and left Ballycastle.[118]

The late Dickie Duffin left school when he was about twelve to work at Portnaloub and these are his recollections after a period of almost 60 years. Dickie's brother, Pat, worked on the winch which was situated on a platform a few feet below the surface. Pat reached Portnaloub by cycling as far as "Marconi's Cottage", then he walked from there. Dickie spent a number of months assisting Pat, winching the buckets up and down the mine shaft. The miners were Willie Duffin, Joe Dillon, Jamie Gallagher, Dan McKiernan and Joe Herrigan. They were employed by John McConville, Reid's business partner, and the mine was referred to as McConville's mine.

The only building at the colliery was a wooden shed, the men took their lunch at the surface sitting round a fire. The coal was taken to Ballycastle by horse and cart, later a boat was used. This was the "Independent", a former lifeboat which had been converted to a motorboat. It was said that this lifeboat had come from H.M.S. Drake, which sank in Church Bay, Rathlin in 1917. John Coll, a Donegal man who was living in Ballycastle was the owner of the "Independent", which was primarily a fishing boat.

Ballycastle man, Paddy McAfee was usually engaged while fishing or boating coal. Within months, however, the boat was wrecked (Sammy Wilkinson supplied the date, 29th July 1921). When the miners finished work each day they left their picks in a particular spot, each man had his own location. One morning, when starting work, they discovered that all their picks had been moved, and this was interpreted as an omen. The men went to work as usual, and were having a tea break when they heard a rumble. The mine where they had been working minutes earlier collapsed, and they had a very lucky escape. There were two mine shafts at Portnaloub, and the one which collapsed was the furthest from Carrickmore, which never reopened.[119]

These two incidents described illustrate vividly the dangers encountered by those working in the mines on a daily basis.

Kelp pit at Carrickmore

A 19th century poem on the mines was set to music and became popular around Ballycastle, but is now forgotten. This was a favourite song of John Clarke, cooper, who died in 1950, his son Seamus recalls two lines of the verse. The song seems to have been generally referred to as "Carrickmore";

"Where Art and Nature does unite, and the cataract does roar,
You will be highly compensated with your vein of Carrickmore."

The vein refers to a seam of iron ore, possibly the seam which became known as McGildowny Black Band. This in turn inspired the small volume of poetry published by John McGuckian in 1992, "The McGildowny Marine Band." The mines inspired another poem by Amergin in 1988, entitled "Moyle Shore, Carrickmore".

Here they worked the sea salt in a pan
By the speckled scree near Portnagree,
And chiseled the ironstone by Srón Bán,
They smelted the ore neath Malawee.

From Malavore and from Corrymeela
Come the colliers to work, with ancient lore
In Griffin, Pollard, far Ballynaveela,
The Neuk, The Deuk, North Star and Carrickmore.

'Twas hard at Falbane in Drumaroan,
Likewise Gobb, the White Mine, green Lagglass,
The Pans, and high Hawk's Nest, Tornaroan
Billy's Shank, old Goldnamuck above the pass.

But the SS Glentow she went down,
In lonely Portaloub – now at ebb,
And the mines they closed all around,
Where dark night now weaves a silent web.

The Culdaff Rock, or Culdaffman, is a reef off Portnaloub, said to have been named after a ship which perished here. This was the reef which claimed the Glentow, dashing the hopes of the people of Ballycastle[119] It was in this area that a brig was wrecked in 1829 with the loss of eight lives.[120] This may in fact refer to the Minerva, a brig which was wrecked in August 1829. Captain James Sawden of Bridlington perished, the survivors were given assistance by Mrs. Conyngham of Bath Lodge.[121] Somewhere off Fair Head, the passenger steamer Falcon perished in a snowstorm during the night of 5th/6th January, 1867. Of the 23 crew and 45 passengers, only three survived. Two bodies were recovered in Ballycastle Bay, others at Murlough.[122] The barque Fawcett bound for Derry from Maryport was wrecked near Carrickmore in March, 1881.[123]

Beyond Portnaloub and close to the shore are the scant remains of some colliers houses, one was inhabited by a family named Dickson.[124] Nearby is a red sandstone building, known locally as Conn's House,[125] which must have served as a coal store (it was not a dwelling). In the 1920's the Birch Tree Mine was to be seen directly below Lough Doo. The old birch has since died and the mine is now buried under massive boulders.[126] Below on the shore is a flat outcrop of rock alongside deep water, identified by Danny McGill as an ideal location for a natural pier.

Nearby is a massive spoil heap, now grassed over and visible from Ballycastle as a grassy ridge. This marks the end of the Ballycastle coalfield as a distinction was always made between this and the Murlough mines.

Murlough

Murlough's secluded bay has attracted visitors from at least the late Stone Age. At Goodland, above Benvan farm, are the foundations of over 100 stone huts, all that remains of an enigmatic Neolithic village.[127] An exploratory investigation of the site was carried out by Professor Estyn Evans over a number of weeks in the mid 1950's.[128] Far below, the ruins of Drumnakill nestle on a ridge along the shore. Pronounced Drumnakeel by locals, the name means church of the ridge. The church was called Kilmologue, and at its Western end Mologue was buried. A number of early Celtic saints were named Mologue, but which one is associated with Murlough is unknown.

Some distance from the church is a bullaun stone (a rock with circular hollows) which served as a baptismal font. Clay removed from St. Mologue's grave by a McCormick was believed to cure certain diseases[129] (the exact position of the grave has now been lost). A similar practice occurred at Diseart near Mount Charles, Co. Donegal, where there are church ruins. In Bonamargy is a grave of one who no doubt was called upon many times to provide clay from Mologue's grave;

HERE   LIETH
THE BODY OF
DANIEL   ROE
Mc COR MICK
OF MURLOCH
WHO   DIED
FEBY 4TH 1800
AGED 74

Daniel and John McCormick who farmed 56 acres at
Knockbrack[130] in 1860 may be of the same family (Murlough lies partly in
Knockbrack townland). There were at least three other families in Carey
who were called Roe, meaning red-haired. They were the McMullans,
Coolnagoppagh, the McLeans of Glenmakeeran and the McNeills of Slipin.
The latter's burial place was Bunamargy, where an 1811 headstone proudly
proclaims Roe in their name.

At one time there were two pilgrimages associated with Murlough,
one approximately three miles long, and a longer circuit of about six miles.
One of the stations was near McBrides bungalow, on the summit of a ridge
between Loughnacranagh and the road. There was once a wooden cross on
the hill, and this replaced an earlier cross, which gave the townland of
Cross its name.[131] Another station was at a cross inscribed stone on a hill
above Murlough called Crockanore.[132] The first station was adjacent to
where the lower carpark is situated at Murlough, and nearby is the
Pilgrim's Port.[133] Further details of the pilgrimage have now been lost, but
nearby are three other ecclesiastical sites which may have been included.
They are the two graveyards in Cross townland, known as Killaleenan and
Killowen respectively (the former is marked Burial Ground for Children on
the 6 inch maps). The third site is another ancient graveyard, also named
Killowen, at E. Torr.

At Ballybradden in Loughguile Parish is a church site called
Kiltoorish, which translates as church of the pilgrimage (Gaelic Cill
Turuis). Not every church held pilgrimages, one can only assume that they
originated due to special devotion to a particular saint. Murlough was a
popular location by the Belfast Naturalists' Field Club for their field trips,
where they often had lunch at the cottage. Some visitors, including John D.
Stewart, Francis Joseph Bigger, Denis Ireland, Sam Hanna Bell, Joseph
Tumelty and Dusty Roads stayed over night in Murlough Cottage.

The Glens poet wrote a number of his poems in an old exercise book, which the late May Stewart preserved. One entitled "The Pride of Murlough Shore" is given here;

The roses bloom in Murlough wood, their blossoms fair to see;
But there's a maid on Murlough braes seems fairer far to me
There's not her equal on the earth, the maid that I adore;
The peerless empress of my heart, the pride of Murlough shore.

Her cheeks are like the roses red that bloom along the brae;
Her lips are like the cherries ripe, that hang on yonder spray
Her bosom like a wreath of snow, the maid that I adore
Alas she's given me nought but woe, the pride of Murlough shore.

Oh, Mary dear my heart is there and ever more shall be
Within my heart thou hast thy shine though ever dear to me
And while life lasts my darling girl, I'll love thee more and more
Would God that I could call thee mine, sweet pride of
Murlough shore.

Telegraphic experiments were carried out by the Royal Navy in 1931-1932, and their personnel were constant visitors to the cottage. The property was sold by the Clarkes in 1932 to the Stewarts, who had fled their native Appin in Argyll. A brief outline of the story is told by Chrissie Laverty in Glynns Volume 10. When the Stewarts arrived at Benvan in the 1750's, there was a Paddy Bheag Scally living here. A field which is yet known as Paddy's Field is named after him.
In recent years Lord Bell, the former merchant seamen and former West Belfast MP Gerry Fitt sought the sanctuary of Murlough Cottage. Today the property and the Benvan farm are owned by the National Trust.[133]

Séan MacBride and Eamon deValera spoke at the inaugural Casement Commemoration at Murlough in 1953. Afterwards they visited Ballycastle and the Cross and Passion College, and a report of their visit featured in the college magazine.

Roger David Casement was born in Dublin, 1864, his father Roger had been a Captain in the Antrim Militia, but resigned rather than participate in evictions. His wife Anne died in 1873, and when Roger died a short time afterwards, their four children were sent to stay at

Magherintemple. Roger was educated at Ballymena until he reached seventeen, when he went to work for a Liverpool shipping company. Later he went to Africa and explored the Congo, then toured America giving lectures on his African adventures. After this, Casement joined the Consular Service, exposing the injustices he had encountered in the Congo and in South America (1910). This humanitarian work earned him a knighthood the following year.

Back in Ireland Casement involved himself in cultural and political activity. He was a prime mover in organizing the first Feis at Waterfoot in 1904, and was involved in the Home Rule meeting held in Ballymoney's Town Hall in October, 1913 (see J.R.B. McMinn's article in Glynns 12). By 1916 Casement was organizing the importation of German weapons, arrested at Banna Strand, Co. Kerry, he was charged with treason and imprisoned in the Tower of London. The trial ended in a guilty verdict, and Casement was sentenced to hang on 3rd August, 1916.

Casement's remains were buried at Pentonville Prison in quick lime. It was not until 1965 that they were released by the Government of the day. This was on condition that the bones were interred at Glasnevin and not as Casement had wished at Murlough. This was because of fears that a grave at Murlough would be used by Republicans to advance their cause. Hundreds of books, articles, pamphlets and plays have been written on Casement, and he was commemorated on two stamps by the Irish Post Office in 1966. A Celtic Cross was erected at the spot chosen for the grave, but this was smashed by Loyalists leaving only the stump of the cross.[134] Casement was a student of Irish history, a dreamer, a romantic, poet, patriot, adventurer, humanitarian and environmentalist. The centenary of his death is in ten years, how will he be remembered then?

The cave at Portnagavna, East of the cottage, was used by smugglers for storing rum and other contraband. The small house known as The Bothy, once a stable,[135] formerly provided accommodation for miners who referred to it as the Miner's Cabin.[136] The earliest recorded coal working at Murlough was by a Dublin merchant, Richard Goodman. He stated in 1761 that he had delivered 20 tons of coal from the bay of "Morlocks" to Dublin.

Arched Mine, Murlough

By 1785, a John Montgomery and Malcolm McNeile were working the coal, which they shipped out in their own 350 ton vessel. William Chapman, an English engineer, was working a mine here in 1790, but because of the difficulties involved he abandoned the project. By June 1791 the colliery was advertised to be let, and again in March 1797.[137] There is a tradition of an English company with the Duke of Devonshire as its chairman, and a manager called McClure, working at Murlough at an unknown date. They erected a wooden bridge to a rock and shipped out their coal.[138]

The ruined house near Portdoo, referred to as the Manager's House, may date from this period as it was in ruins by the 1830's.

Ruins of the managers house

Window of Manager's house, photo by Mary Chambers

Richard Griffith, who surveyed Murlough in 1817, stated in 1829 that coal had not been worked here for many years. The workings were of considerable extent, the upper level was called the White Mine, and the lower was "Good Man's Vein". Chapman, an engineer of great talent, worked the upper bed of blind coal which was 2 foot 6 inches thick, but shipping the coal posed enormous problems.[139]

The mines appear to have been idle throughout most of the 19th century. About 1878 T.B. Marshall was working the coal here, and by 1893 a man named Jamieson was involved. The coal was shipped out in small boats from the Stage Rock, which provided deep water.[140] Local tradition is that the coal was shipped from a rounded black rock, known as the Ring Stone, so called because of its mooring ring. This rock is at times submerged which would have posed problems.[141] John Reid from Dublin visited Murlough in 1918 and decided to take a lease of the mines. He commenced work with three or four men exploring the old adits into the Arched Mine and the White Mine.[142]

The White Mine Coal is the highest seam, 2 foot 9 inches thick, bituminous, and described as fairly good house coal. This coal was selling in Ballycastle in April, 1919 at £2-10-0 (£2.50) per ton, which included £1 cartage. Some coal was sent off by rail to Ballymoney. Because of the high cost of cartage and the difficulty of obtaining carts, the venture was not very profitable, and was abandoned in June, 1921.[143]

Later, James Delargy, Glenballyeamon, leased the mines as a source of coal to supply his limeworks. John Hill, a Carey man now residing in Ballycastle, was a miner at Murlough in the 1930's. He started working aged twelve, with his father Ned, an experienced miner, and these are his recollections. One day during lunch break John saw a rat and he made a swipe at it with a pick. Ned observed this and told him to let the rat be. John naturally thought that his father was joking, but soon realized that he wasn't. "Why?" he asked, and was told that this was a safety measure. When rats are seen leaving a mine, then it is time to get out fast, as a roof collapse is imminent. This did in fact occur about 1937 when the rats, described as being very tame, were seen fleeing the mine. The men got out and shortly afterwards there was a collapse of approximately 50 tons of material. After the rubble was cleared away the men went back to work, as if nothing had happened.

An old model T Ford lorry known as "Roaring Meg", with bus tyres and a cab with no doors, was driven by a man known as Knowles. This vehicle which could transport two tons of coal ended its days at Murlough, abandoned there as a rusting hulk. Steel hutches which held approximately a half ton of coal were used in the mine, and the explosives were kept in a partially opened mine on higher ground. The local men went home by climbing the cliff slopes at the spot known as the Farragans. There were sallies growing here which the men grabbed as they hauled themselves up, to a home made ladder and over the cliff.[144]

The other workers stayed in Murlugh Cottage and the Bothy. Those who worked to Delargy in the early days at Murlough included Dan McKiernan, Tornaroan, Jamie McMullan, Slipin, James McAlister, Losset, was a charge hand who later worked in the English mines; Dan McAlister, brother of James, Joe McCarry, Clare Street Ballycastle. Daniel Butler, Bob and Jamie Butler, Ballyvoy, the latter lived at The Lawn, and drove the Model T Ford at Murlough; Johnny Rankin, Drumaridley, Willie Birt, a native of Glenravel met and married a Carry woman; Eddie Hill, a brother of John Hill, worked at Murlough for a brief period; Jamie and George O'Brien, brothers from Glenravel, Harry McMullan, Skerry.[145]

Jamie Davidson, Drumnakeel, worked three years in the mines, and these are his recollections. This was an anthracite mine, the coal face was approximately seven feet wide and the mine was a dry one. Two old miners from the Glenravel area, Jamie O'Brien and Harry McMullan lodged in The Bothy. They would "hole the coal" by excavating the underlying shale to a depth of about three feet. As they progressed they crawled in further until all you saw were their feet sticking out. The foreman, James McAllister, then bored holes in the coal and placed the charges, a stick and a half in each borehole. They were then plugged with clay and the mine was evacuated before the charges were fired. No one was permitted to enter the mine for fifteen minutes after firing had occurred, as a safety precaution, but this was not always adhered to. One man went back in early on one occasion and suffered a head injury when he was hit by some material.

Jamie's job was to fill the hutches with the coal brought down by blasting, then he and Ned Mullan pushed the hutches to the mine entrance. This required being totally focused when steering as a hutch could easily be derailed, with dangerous consequences. Pushing out the hutches was strenuous work, and was especially tiring on the legs. At the mouth of the mine, the hutches were tipped onto a zinc chute. While the coal was being removed, the two miners worked on another coal face. The excavated shale was piled up alongside the rails.

Regular inspections were carried out on the roof of the mine by probing with the shaft end of a pick. If a boast sound was heard then a pit prop would be inserted, and the men would "crown" it with a cross bar. There were a number of circular rock formations known as "pot lids" on the roof of the mine. Once the miners excavated one, revealing it was only three inches deep.

The miners were supplied with picks and carabine lamps, which clipped on to their helmets. They paid for the carabine, which cost about six pence per tin, and two tins were used in a 5½ day week. Work finished at one o'clock on Saturdays. In the Winter months the men took their tea breaks within the mine, but in the Summer they sat outside at the entrance to the Arched Mine. Tea was made from the spring water which poured out in a stream at the limestone rocks.

The coal was loaded onto lorries up at the North Gate, where the carpark is today. Once a lorry went over the edge, but miraculously there were no injuries to the driver or anyone else. The incident shocked Jamie however; he says that he did not sleep for weeks afterwards. Willie Colville from Skerry and Mick McKeown who hurled for Cushendall were lorry drivers. The men often observed the Kelly coalboats as they passed by on their way to and from Coleraine. When conditions were favourable the boats waited at an inlet to catch the flood tide as this surge of water propelled the boats along.

Jamie went home up through the hazels and over the cliff from where he walked to Coolanlough. Here he collected his bicycle for the last leg of his journey home to Drumnakeel. (Jake and Marie Patterson operate their popular Drumnakeel Herb Garden and Tea Room from Jamie's old home). When the mine at Murlough closed, Jamie was transferred to Blackpark mine, his wages were then £5 per week. A number of other local men who worked at Murlough included John McFall (Big John), Ballyucan; Johnny Rankin, Junior, John Murphy, John McConnell, Senior was book keeper; Paddy McGowan; Hugh McNeill[146] and Lawrence McHenry, Ballyvoy. The latter worked at the Ballyvoy pit, the White Mine and also for a period in an open cast mine in Yorkshire.[147]

John and Tom McCarthy were two Glenravel men who worked at Murlough. The McMullans from Carnlough were employed by Jamie Delargy in his early days at Murlough to draw the coal. The only reason Delargy got involved in mining was to supply his limeworks with coal. The lime was spread on farms in an area from Clough, The Braid, Broughshane, Ballymena, Ballycarry and Islandmagee, where Willie Peoples is recalled as a good customer. The Glenballyeamon limeworks ceased operating in 1966, and eleven years later Jamie Delargy died on 31st May 1977.[148]

To the East of Drumnakill a number of trial pits were opened but of their history, nothing is known. One was at Legatrummon, but even this place-name is now obsolete. Ligahapple (hollow of the mare) and Lignabodagh (hollow of the old man) are both East of Benvan (the white peak). Ruebane means white point, and the Red Brae is named from the red soil which is exposed in landslides. The Councillor's Plantation is near McCarry's farmhouse. The Doon is a grassy mound near The Bothy, and nearby is McDonnell's Port, and Net Port. The latter place-name is a translation from the Gaelic, as is the Lookout Rock at Benvan. Smugglers used the cave at Portnagoma when they brought in rum and other commodities. Crockanore, translated as hill of gold, but there is no tradition here to explain the origin of the name.[149]

Locals fished glashan and lythe from the rocks, until recently the bait was boiled mashed potatoes and sometimes barley was added. Two men who fished here regularly were Pat McAuley and John McGill, who died in 1959. Another local once caught a salmon, which had been attracted by the scent of fresh water.[150]

Murlough is a sheltered location for sea anglers, although there are ebb tides and counter tides here. Many local families have fished at Murlough over the generations, 13 boats are recalled here in the 1960's. Jamie Stewart of Benvan, Pat McBride of Ballyreagh and the Scallys of Ballyucan all fished but no more, and the shore is now largely deserted.[151] Patrick Scally, Crockbrack, recorded as a fisherman in 1866, may have been one of that family who traded butter and eggs with schooners in the bay. The tradition is that on occasions payment was a bottle of whiskey.[152]

The Clarkes of Murlough were skilled craftsmen who could build and repair boats. The "Murlough Rose" was one of their boats which competed successfully in a number of regattas.[153] The Clarkes were at one time agents to the Earl of Antrim, and the collected the rents of the tenant farmers. Murlough children attended Ballyucan School, which had been established by Lord Antrim to provide education for his tenant's families. Lord Antrim appointed the teachers, maintained the school, and he also built a teachers residence at nearyby Dooey Plantation. The school consisted of two large classrooms, one for the junior pupils, and the other for seniors, each with its own teacher. After the sale of the Antrim facilities in the 1930's, the school came under jurisdiction of the Antrim County Educational Committee.

Ballyucan School, 1995

When Ballyucan School closed c1974, the remaining pupils on the rolls transferred to Barnish Primary School, Ballyvoy. The roll call of teachers who taught at Ballyucan over the years included Sally Osborne (nee McGrath), Mary McDonnell (nee McErlain), Kathleen McCarry, Colliers Hall, John Duffin, Ballycastle, and a male teacher named McCambridge who died tragically.[154] Another male teacher named Whyte transferred to Rasharkin (a grandson is Jude Whyte, Belfast). Master Moore was a Kerryman who was a prime mover in the establishment of Carry Faughs hurling club in 1904. He married a Gillan of Losset, and the couple emigrated in 1910 to America.[155] Master Moore became an attorney in America, and he returned on a holiday on at least one occasion. His wife was killed during the Prohibition.[156]

The best remembered of Ballyucan's teachers was John Henry Cullen, who was said to have been born in Armagh City.[157] Others said that he was a native of the Boyne area, and that he spent almost 70 years in the Ballycastle area. What is known is that he was teaching at Ballyucan by 1894,[158] and that he married Maggie McHenry, whose family operated the Ballyvoy Post Office. After a number of years at Ballyucan School, Cullen transferred to a school at Fairhill Street, Ballycastle.

John Henry was a great conversationalist, a staunch Nationalist, keen walker and angler. He walked with a short but brisk step, and anyone walking beside him invariable found themselves lagging behind.[159] Master Cullen taught at night classes and gave refresher courses for policemen, the late Paddy Barton (who served with the police in Palestine) recalled. The Cullens are buried at Carey Chapel, appropriately along the wall which forms the boundary with Barnish School. John Henry Cullen died on 7th October 1950, his wife Margaret died 13th July 1932, a son Patrick Joseph died 11th December 1954, and a daughter Margaret died 14th April 1965.

Beyond Ballyucan lies Torr, called Toretowne in 1669 when 13 householders were recorded by the Hearth Money Rolls. This was a tax on hearths from which the poor were exempt, and indeed some houses had no hearths. As only the heads of the households were recorded it follows that the population was then considerably larger. The names of those recorded in 1669 were McCloe, Miller (3), McCurdy, McAllister, McCollum, McCaie (McKay), O'Kennan, McAtulle, Stewart, O'Hart and Johnson.[160]

Torr salmon fishery was held in 1860 by a John Reany who resided in East Torr, where he farmed 21 acres, 3 roads and 5 perches.[161] The Torr fishery was never a very productive one until someone discovered that the net was not in the best strategic position. A change was made and this gave a better yield. The spot where the salmon was sighted, known as "the sight", was along the shore, and not on the head as one would have expected. Salmon caught at Torr were stored in the ice-house, a round roofed building by the roadside at the Ice-house Brae.[162] This placename also occurs at Knocksoghey, Ballintoy and Moville, Co. Donegal.

A Ballycastle guide pre 1943 has the following advertisement:

Torr Head
Salmon Fishery and Tea Rooms
(8 miles from Ballycastle)
To reach Torr Head follow Telephone Poles from Ballyvoy
See the Salmon Caught – Eat Them
Scenery unsurpassed for Grandeur
Boating, Bathing, Sea and Trout Fishing
Charming Glen and Waterfall within 10 minutes walk
G.T. Macartney, Proprietor

George Travers McCartney died at Glengarrif, Co. Cork, 11th July 1943. He was the owner of the Torr Head fishery and was responsible for organising the regattas and sports at Torr.[163]

The late Jamie Davidson had treasured memories of Torr's gala day. The Sports were held on McLister's farm on the same day as the Regatta, generally a Wednesday. All the events were free to enter and were well supported by people from the surrounding area. Events included horseshoe throwing, athletic races, bicycle races, tug-of-war and the greasy pole. The latter event was unique, with a pole up to 16 feet cast out over the water. At the end of the pole was the prize, a small pig suspended by its legs which were securely tied. Anyone who could reach the pig, untie the animal and bring it back could keep the prize. Walking on the pole was not permitted, instead one slid along by using hands and feet. Many men tried to claim the pig, but all were unsuccessful and a few ended up in the water, much to the delight of the spectators.

Bob Dillon and Johnny McKeague are recalled participating in the athletic events and one of the organising committee was Lochy McAfee. Cigarettes, food and drink were sold in a tent in the corner of the field. Stout sold at 7 pence a bottle and whiskey cost 10 pence (old money). The days events ended with a dance held in the McLister's big barn. Jamie recalled leaving one dance at 5.00 am; he cycled home, changed his clothes, then went to work, "thinning turnips". Rathlin born Neill McCouaig won the 1938 Regatta and the following year he won again. The cups which were presented by the McCartney family, are today in the possession of Neill's son Lawrence.

In the severe winter of 1947-8, the people of Torr were cut off by road from the outside world and food was in short supply. Jack Coyles, Ballycastle, bought a boatload of provisions, which included milk from Dhu Varren Dairies, Portrush, around Fair Head to relieve the residents of Torr.[165]

Smuggling, once widespread, had ceased by the mid 1830's, it was said due to the 12 coastguards then stationed in the parish.[166] The contraband which passed between the Antrim and Argyll coasts included sugar, tea, tobacco, salt, spirits, whiskey and whisky, soap, corn, cattle, hides, horses and wool.[167]

Beyond Torr is the Green Hill and the townland of Aughnaholle, which is translated at field of the wool or fleeces. This may well be evidence of where the wool was smuggled on pre-arranged nights. Griffith's Valuation includes two names at East Torr which are not local and may have arrived as Coastguards. They are James Parkin and Thomas Cullary, both surnames have since died out.

The details of a few Coastguards culled from various sources are given here; Hamilton Keown, Coastguard, his son William married Martha McCormick in Culfeightrin Church, 3rd December 1845. Hamilton's wife Margaret died 21st November 1861; he is recorded at Castle Street in the Griffith Valuation.

William and Martha Keown resided at Thorn Cottage, their daughter Annie Jane married Henry Shepherd in Culfeightrin Parish Church, November 1866. A William Shepherd, H.M.S. Duncan, died in the West Indies, 12th August 1865 aged 19. He is commemorated by a headstone in Culfeightrin churchyard. Wm. Keown, late Chief Boatman, died 9th January 1930, aged 70 and is buried at St. James'. John Nancollis, Chiefboatman, Murlough, his son John died 1st July 1852, aged 22, buried Culfeightrin.

James Harry, a native of St. Ives, Cornwall, late Chief Officer of Coastguards, died at Ballycastle, 7th January 1876, aged 76, buried Culfeightrin. William Elliot, aged 38, Coastguard at Torr, married Mary Robinson, 24, Ballycastle. The couple wed in Culfeightrin Church, 9th December, 1864, her father Daniel Robinson was a Ballycastle Coastguard. Neill Sergeant, pilot at Torr Head, his son John was a Coastguard Boatman, who married Elizabeth Thompson in Culfeightrin Parish Church, 27th December 1847. Elizabeth was the daughter of Dan Thompson, Coastguard Boatman of Layde Parish.

Hugh McIvor, Drumahitt, retired Coastguard, his wife Sarah died 10th June 1873, aged 70, buried Carey Chapel. This family who also spelt their name as McKeever were related to the late Mary McAuley, Kenbane. Denis McLaughlin and John McGuire were Coastguards at Torr during the mid 1820's.

The McListers of Torr are said to be descended from a Scottish Coastguard, and that their name was changed from McAllister.[168] Alexander McLyster c1861 had a house with 22 acres, 1 road and 5 perches leased at

East Torr.[169] The late Joe Pill, Ballycastle, his father was a Coastguard who had been transferred to Torr from Ballywalter, Co. Down.[170] The Torr Coastguards were involved in an incident during the troubled period of September, 1920.

"Torr Head Coastguard station was visited by 50 armed raiders on Saturday night who held up the guard, and eventually decamped with 5 revolvers, 300 rounds of ammunition, 4 telescopes, 2 binoculars and a large quantity of service gear. The raid was carried out about 11 o'clock and must have been carefully planned as both the Coastguard and the signalling station, which is situated 200 yards from the main building, were visited simultaneously. "The only person in the signalling station was the look-out man ... the raiders dismantled the telescope, were very polite and their leader spoke with a cultivated accent. None of the garrison was molested, and no effort was made to visit their sleeping apartments of the station. It was afterwards discovered that the wires to Ballycastle had been cut."[171]

Ice-house, Torr with Coastguard Station ruins in background

This was followed up the following Wednesday by about 40 military in 3 lorries who raided a number of premises in Ballycastle. No arms were discoved but a local garage had three cars dismantled and their permits removed.[172]

Torr was an important signalling station during World War One but was due to be decommissioned at the time of the raid. In fact all the equipment and stores had been packed awaiting removal by a trawler. Then early Saturday morning 6th November the vacant station was set alight by incendiaries and was destroyed.[173] The watch-house was spared this fate and survived as an Auxiliary Coastguard Lookout until comparatively recently, when it became a private dwelling.

Although the views in all directions are spectacular, the building today stands derelict, a grim sentinel to the ravages of vandals.

This is an ancient site – in the Middle Ages beacon fires blazed whenever aid was required.[174]

Along this stretch of the coast there are a number of small ports. Murlough has already been mentioned, and in West Torr there are Portadoon, Escort Port and Portnadig. South of Torr are Portaleen, Portnathalin, Portmore and Portnahorna. A local man recalled when there were six fishing boats kept in one of these little creeks, in 1993 there were none.[175]

Portnahorna signifies port of the oats, where corn was smuggled out at opportune periods, mainly in the 1770's and 1780's.[176] Portnathalin has been translated as port of the salt,[177] this was another commodity which was smuggled from the Glens to Scotland. There is at present no evidence of salt having been manufactured at Portnathalin, as there was elsewhere in the parish.

Portaleen, which is adjacent to the Torr salmon fishery, could be interpreted as port of the net (but other translations are possible).[178] At Culdaff in Inishowen there is another place named Portaleen. Escort Port is so named as it was where people from Escort fished from. Escort was once a clachan of a considerable number of houses which were known as "Little Dublin".[179]

In the 19th century Torr had its own public house, its site is now the picnic area near the Green Hill. The publican is said to have emigrated

Coastguard Station ruins from Torr

with his family, even their surname has now been forgotten.[180] Torr also at one time had its own hurling team, they played in a field near the shore.[181]

Oral tradition relates that a local thatcher who worked around Southend in Kintyre in the 19th century used Torr as his departure point for Scotland.[182] This was almost certainly Hector McIlfatrick, known as Heckie, who died in Ballycastle in the 1890's. Hector composed the song "The Thatchers of Glenrae", which is well known around Kintyre. Glenrae is now a forested area near the hill of Cnoc Odhar above Glenbreckerie, North of Carskey Bay.[183] The song describes how after a bad experience working in Glenrae, the thatchers returned to Ballycastle. But as the wages were low the men decided that they would go back to Kintyre, but not to Glenrae.[184]

Inland from Torr where the old road to Cushendun ends in a track over the mountain is the Hungry House. Situated in Ballyvennaght townland, the house was in existence by the 1830's.[185] The name appears to have originated from the fact that weary travellers on reaching this point were usually very hungry. There is no tradition to suggest any other reason for the name.

Along the main Ballycastle road at Craigagh Wood is a small abandoned dwelling known as the Hungry House.[186] A third house in North Antrim with this name was located at Evishnacrow near Parkmore. This house, in ruins by the 1930's, was like the Ballyvennaght house near an abandoned stretch of roadway.

Chapter Two References

1. McCahan Scrapbook
2. By The Moyle Shore, Vol. One p16
3. Geology of North Antrim, pp 3,4. McCahan
4. Letters concerning the Northern Coast of the County of Antrim. Rev. Wm. Hamilton
5. Glynns Vol. 33, p102
6. Andy McLernon (deceased), Ballycastle
7. John Hill, Macauley Park, Ballycastle
8. Mick McAuley, Ballyvoy
9. Dickie Duffin
10. Joe Butler, Ballyvoy
11. McCahan's Local Histories, Chapter B, pp 2,6
12. R. Griffith
13. John McAuley, Manchester; Dan Duncan (deceased)
14. Dickie Duffin
15. Andy McKinley
16. John McAuley, Manchester
17. Glynns 16, Vol. 17
18. Jamie McKiernan (deceased)
19. Jack Coyles
20. Dickie Duffin
21. David Dillon (deceased), Lisburn, formerly Ballycastle
22. McCahan's scrapbook
23. Chronicle, 4/7/1998
24. David Dillon and Paddy Clarke
25. Glynns Vol 17, p27, article by Danny McGill
26. Dickie Duffin
27. Glynns Vol. 1, pp 11,14
28. Griffith Valuation, p52
29. Ulster Surnames, p202, by Robert Bell, Blackstaff Press, Belfast, 1988
30. Geology of North Antrim, pp 2,6, by Robert McCahan
31. The scrapbook is presently held by the Presbyterian Historical Society, Belfast
32. Seamus Clarke
33. Andy McLernon (deceased)
34. Mick McAuley, Junior, Blackpark Road, Ballyvoy
35. Chronicle, 5/11/1887

36. Hugh A. Boyd (deceased)
37. Jamie Davidson (deceased)
38. Dickie Duffin (deceased)
39. Jamie Davidson (deceased), who was one of the workmen
40. Dickie Duffin, his sisters Cassie O'Connor and Maggie Campbell (all deceased)
41. John Holbrook, Ballycastle
42. John McAuley, Manchester
43. Dickie Duffin
44. John Holbrook
45. Mick McAuley, Ballyvoy
46. Jack Coyles and Jamie Davidson
47. Dickie Duffin and Jamie Davidson
48. McCahan's Local Histories, Chapter B, p6
49. Pat McBride, Ballyreagh
50. Place-Names of Northern Ireland, Volume Seven, p183
51. Jack Coyles and Dickie Duffin
52. Stewarts of Ballintoy, pp 50,51
53. Wilson p172
54. Jamie Davidson
55. John McKeague, Ballynagard, who was informed by his father
56. Griffith Valuation, pp 55,58
57. Document in the Greer, Hamilton Gailey office, Ballymoney
58. David Dillon (deceased), Lisburn, formerly Ballycastle
59. St. Patricks Church brochure
60. Ulster Journal of Archaeology, January 1905
61. Danny McGill, Ballinlea
62. R. Griffith
63. Dickie Duffin, John Hill and Mick McAuley
64. Fiachra MacGabhann personal communication
65. Grand Jury Presentation Book for County Antrim, Lent Assizes, 1817, p36
66. Robert McCahan scrapbook
67. McCahan's Local Histories, Chapter B, p11
68. Dickie Duffin
69. Rosina McAuley and Ellen O'Kane (deceased)
70. Joe Lyden and Dickie Duffin
71. Dickie Duffin
72. John McAuley
73. Dickie Duffin
74. John McAuley

75. Dickie Duffin
76. Jamie Davidson
77. Dominic Darragh
78. Jamie McKiernan (deceased)
79. Jamie Davidson
80. Dickie Duffin, who was informed by his father
81. Jamie McKiernan
82. R. Griffith, 1829, p65
83. Glynns 12, pp 29,32
84. Wilson, p66
85. McCahan, Chapter B, p7
86. Glynns Vol. 16, p17
87. Glynns Vol. 12, p31
88. Cutting in McCahan's scrapbook
89. Joyce, "The Origin and History of Irish names of Places", 3
90. McCahan, Chapter B, p6
91. Ulster Journal of Archaeology, Vol. 1, 1938
92. McCahan, Chapter B, pp 7,8
93. The Chronicle
94. Pat McBride (deceased), Ballyreagh
95. Jamie Davidson
96. Coleraine Chronicle
97. Coleraine Chronicle
98. Hull p264
99. McCahan, Chapter B, pp 13,14
100. Jack Coyle and Dickie Duffin, both deceased
101. John Hill
102. The Harsh Winds of Rathlin, p25, by Tommy Cecil, Rathlin Island. Impact Printing, Ballycastle, 1990
103. P.J. Dallat & Sons, Funeral Directors, 1891-1991, p13, by Cahal Dallat, J.P., B.A., D.A.S.E., M.Phil., Hon. D. Litt.
104. Cecil, p72
105. McCahan scrapbook
106. Dickie Duffin
107. McCahan scrapbook
108. Dickie Duffin, Jack Coyle
109. John and Patsy Hill, Drumawillan, Ballycastle
110. Hugh A. Boyd, who was informed by Capt. Humphries
111. McCahan scrapbook
112. Coleraine Chronicle, 13/10/1888
113. Dickie Duffin

114. Coleraine Chronicle, 14/8/1858
115. MickMcAuley, Ballyvoy
116. Griffith, p76
117. Ireland's Own, 26/3/1999, article by Willie O'Kane
118. McCahan
119. Recollections of Dickie Duffin, speaking in 1988
120. Derry and Anrtim Year Book
121. E-Mail from Gary Fudge to John McKeegan,
     Ballycastle Library, 10/10/2003
122. Dalriada p116, William Adams, 1906. Reprint by Causeway
     Books, Bushmills, 2004
123. Shipwrecks Of The Ulster Coast, p152. Ian Wilson,
     Impact Amergin, 1979
124. Seamus Clarke and the late Dan Duncan
125. Dominic Darragh
126. Dickie Duffin
127. Jon Marshall
128. Chrissie Laverty, Ballycastle, formerly Murlough
129. McCahan, Chapter E, p6
130. Griffith's Valuation, p58
131. Pat McBride (deceased), Ballyreagh
132. Pat Dennis, Coolnagoppagh
133. Chrissie Laverty
134. Seamus Clarke
135. Chrissie Laverty
136. Dickie Duffin
137. Wilson, pp 84,85
138. McCahan, Chapter B, p17
139. Griffith, p77
140. Wright, p77
141. Sammy Wilkinson
142. Cutting dated 5/10/1918, from McCahan scrapbook
143. McCahan
144. John Hill, Macauley Park, Ballycastle
145. John Hill, Mick McAuley, Maggie Campbell (deceased),
     Ballycastle, J McVeigh, Carey Mill, Sean Delargy, Glenballyeamon,
     and Alex Fyfe
146. Jamie Davidson, born 16/6/1909, died December 2004
147. Lawrence McHenry, Ballyvoy
148. Sean Delargy, Glenballyeamon
149. Chrissie Laverty

150. Jamie Davidson, and Paddy McNeill, Boyd Court, Ballycastle
151. Mick McAuley, Ballyvoy
152. Sammy Wilkinson, Ballintoy, who was informed by Johnny Scally, The Warren, Broughanlea (both now deceased)
153. Dickie Duffin
154. Chrissie Laverty
155. Ambrose Hunter (deceased)
156. Billy Boylan, Greenans, Glenshesk
157. Hugh A. Boyd
158. Slater's Directory, p22
159. Ambrose Hunter (who was taught by J.H. Cullen)
160. Glynns Vol. One, p14
161. Griffith p47
162. Sammy Wilkinson
163. Loughguile A Parish and its people, p52, 1993. Hugh McLean, "Cill Turuis", Ballybraddan, Loughguile
164. Lawrence McCouaig, Market Street, Ballycastle
165. Danny McGill, Ballinlea, who was informed by the late Jack Coyles
166. Glynns Vol. 5, p53
167. Glynns Vol. 4, pp 36-46
168. Andy McKinley, Ballycastle, and Henry Joe McHenry (both deceased)
169. Griffith Valuation, p48
170. Seamus Clarke (deceased)
171. Irish Telegraph, 13/9/1920 (front page)
172. Irish Telegraph, 16/9/1920
173. McCahan
174. Glynns 2, pp 8,25
175. Henry Joe McHenry (deceased)
176. Glynns Vol 4, p40
177. Place-Names of Northern Ireland, p203
178. Place-Names of Northern Ireland, p202
179. Danny McGill, Ballinlea
180. Mary Meeke, and her late husband Harry
181. Dickie Duffin
182. Jack Coyles
183. Glynns Vol. 6, p19
184. Glynns
185. Grand Jury Presentation Book for County Antrim, Lent Assizes, 1836, p180
186. Dickie Duffin

CHAPTER THREE

FAIRHEAD TO THE ENCHANTED ISLAND

The East side of Ballycastle Bay is flanked by the great mass of Fair Head, formerly called Benmore. The latter has traditionally been translated as the large peak, but another possible meaning is majestic peak, which is perhaps more fitting. The whole area is resplendent with archaeological and historical remains with a crannog, cairns, ecclesiastical sites, forts, mines, Coolanlough clachan and other miscellaneous features. Doomore dominates the skyline above Carrickmore, and is clearly visible from Ballycastle promenade.

Excavation of the site revealed evidence of Norman occupation from c1180 to the 14th century. Artefacts uncovered included part of a cross inscribed rotary quern, flint scrapers, 2 fragments of green glaze of 13th – 14th date, animal bones, and a bloom of iron. The latter showed that iron was smelted on the site. Traces of a stone pavement were also uncovered.[1]

Coolanlough, Fairhead

Lough na Cranagh

A much earlier structure is the well known crannog of Lough na Cranagh. Crannogs are man made islands which date from the Bronze Age period. They were defensive by design, access was by canoe, or in some cases an underwater causeway. The Fair Head crannog has evidence of three landing places, with the nearest one approximately fifty yards from the shore. Around the crannog the water varies in depth from 18 inches to 20 feet.[2]

Other known crannog sites in N. Antrim include Loughlynch, Mosside; Ballylough, Bushmills; Lissanoure, Loughguile; and Ballywillan Bog, Portrush. In the Fair Head area there are a number of forts which are often indicated in place-names which contain lis, cashel doon, dun and rath. At the ecclesiastical site of Killaleenan in Cross townland there was a cashel which was a massive circular dry stone structure. Dunmakeltar is a townland which took its name from the fort of Cealtchar's son.[3] Adjacent is Drumadoon townland which means fort of the ridge and here during a three month excatavion in 2003, a bronze bell shrine was discovered. Described as one of the most important archaeological finds ever made during an excavation in Ireland, this is the subject of two articles in The Glynns, Volume 32, 2004. Lisnacalliagh in Ballyreagh Upper townland appears at face value to mean fort of the hag or old woman. But the local pronunciation is Lisnakilly and this spelling occurs on a headstone of 18.

Doonmore from Coolanlough

Lisnakilly may mean fort of the churches and there are two sites within a short distance. Lisnacalliagh was removed by James McIlroy to make a stackyard a short time after the end of the Great War. Carvadoon in Ballyvennaght townland signifies quarterland of the fort. Elsewhere in this general area there were forts at Barnish, Ballyreagh and Drumnakeel.

Lough na Crannagh

Religious Sites

At Craigfad there is what appears to be another fort, but the enclosure has been identified by Jon Marshall as a water worship ritual site.[4] A more common feature is the holy well where the original Druidic site has been adopted by the early Celtic church. On John Darragh's farm at Doon is Toberdoney which means the Sunday well as it was the custom to visit this well on a Sunday. The well was said to be effective in the cure of eye complaints and before leaving it was the practice to place a stone here. At one time there were about four trailer loads of stones at the well showing the large numbers of people who came seeking a cure.[5]

There are at least seven other holy wells in Co. Antrim named Toberdoney. The one at Cloughmills was recently tidied up and given a new lease of life as part of a community development scheme.[6] Adjacent to the former Ballyucan school there was a holy well which was visited by large numbers of people in the pre famine period.[7] The name of the well has long since been forgotten, as this spot has been known as The Gate from at least the 1830s. Killaleenan is an early ecclesiastical site in Cross townland and close to the Craigfad boundary There are the foundations of a church here "filled with graves of unbaptised children".[8] The O.S. 6" map marks the site as "burial ground for children".

121

Still born and children who died unbaptised were formerly buried in particular graveyards, often in unconsecrated ground. Old forts were on occasion used as children's graveyards which are known throughout Ireland and also in Scotland. There are approximately fifteen examples in Culfeightrin civil parish, a larger number than most parishes. In Carey however most if not all of the children's graveyards appear to have been consecrated sites, old abandoned graveyards.

Killaleenan is recorded c1860 as containing 20 perches of ground.[9] Along the upper (east) side of the old Ballycastle/Cushendun road at Drumadoon is Kilpatrick which contained 6 perches c1860.[10] The site marked on O.S. maps as "Grave Yd. for Children" is near where the Drumadoon bell shrine was discovered in 2003. Adjacent to the Drumnakeel Herb and Tea Garden is a standing stone which stands in a children's graveyard. This was formerly much larger as human remains have been discovered in an adjacent field known as the Keel Field.[11]

Drumnakeel means ridge of the church. Jamie Davidson who was born in the adjacent cottage recalled the graveyard in his youth. The burial ground was enclosed by a circular stone wall, topped with barbed wire. Entry to the enclosure was through a wooden gate, which was kept locked and the key held by the county council. On two different occasions Jamie was called upon by the local undertaker to bury an infant here. The undertaker arrived with a small white coffin then departed again. Jamie dug a grave and interred the remains, his payment was five shillings (25p). There were no clergy nor anyone else present. These were the last ever interments in the centuries old graveyard. One day a man arrived carrying a coffin which held an infant's remains. He knocked on Jamie's door and said that he wished to bury his infant at Drumnakeel. But after a discussion with Jamie the man left and went elsewhere.

Bonamargy

Jamie recalled having to bury an infant at Bonamargy in the area known as the Poor Ground and again his payment was five shillings. He worked as a guide and caretaker at the friary for 18 years. One of his tasks was to flag the floor of the gate lodge where the Black Nun lived. He also flagged the floor of the day room and attended a Belfast stone mason who built a wall at the West gate. The stone came from a quarry in Co. Down. A few years ago a decision was taken to demolish this wall as the material was not local stone. The friary is build of sandstone with a mortar of lime and it is said ox blood. Tradition relates that the day room was roofed over by filling the room with earth which was compacted down hard. The stone roof was built on this material which was removed when the roof had set.[12]

Bonamargy Friary

Dickie Duffin recalled burying a number of stillborn infants at night in a corner next to the wall of the Poor Ground. Before the Great War no headstones were permitted in this area of the graveyard. After a number of service men were interred here they were commemorated with headstones. Then when 64 year old Alex Hamill died in October 1929 a collection was made in Ballycastle to pay for his burial and funeral. The amount raised was over subscribed and after paying the woman who washed the corpse, a small headstone was erected to his memory.

Alex Hamill lived in Davey's Row off Clare Street and died single. He is recalled working on the renovation of what is now the Anzac Bar some time in the early 1900's.[13] There were formerly a Hamill family living in Carey and Alex may have been of this stock. His headstone which was the first that one met on entering the graveyard has now fallen and is hidden from view.

Bonamargy was one of at least 44 friaries of the Third Order of Francisans regular established in Ireland between the 1420's and the dissolution of the monastries in 1537. The Third Order flourished in Ireland, especially in the less anglicized areas of Ulster and Connacht.[14] The earliest known Third Order friary in Ireland was at Killeenbreenan,

Co. Mayo established several years prior to 1428. Glenarm Francisan Friary was founded in 1445.[15] Under the monastic Rule of Hospitality friaries were obliged to provide food and lodging to anyone who came to the gate seeking such.

Education was another important aspect of the friars, not only as tutors to noble families but they also sought to educate the poor.[16] Oral tradition was that the friary at Bonamargy was to have been built at Kilmoyle, the site of an ancient graveyard in the Grange of Drumtullagh but for some reason long since forgotten there were a change of plans in favour of Bonamargy.[17] Rory McQuillan has been largely credited with Bonamargy's foundation about the year 1500 but this has been disputed. Both the McDonnells and the McCormicks claim the honour, the latter state that one of their chieftans Phelim was the founder.[18]

There is a local tradition of English soldiers being billeted at Bonamargy in 1584 when they stabled their horses within the friary. The natives met and discussed how they could end the sacrilegious occupation visited upon them. They decided on a night attack and their first objective was to kill the sentry on duty. Next they blocked all the friary windows and doors using headstones at the latter. When this was achieved the thatched roof was then set alight. In the inferno that followed all the English and their horses perished.[19] A slightly different version was current in the 1830's when the local families that participated in the attack were then remembered. They were McDonnell, McNeill, McAllister, McGildowney, McAuley, McAfee and McCormick.[20] The friary was repaired again and services were resumed.

About the year 1600 the prior was named as O'Dornan.[21] Between 1619 and 1646 Bonamargy was the base for the Irish Franciscan Mission to the Higlands and Western Isles. The Scots came in increasing numbers to receive the sacraments and Bonamargy became for a period a second Iona.[22] Upwards of 500 Scots were being received into the church annually at Bonamargy, at one period before the Mission there had only been one priest in Scotland. He was the Franciscan John Ogilvie. The last large scale confirmation ceremony took place in 1639 performed by Bonaventure Magennis the Franciscan Bishop of Down and Connor. As many as 1,000 people are stated to have crossed over to Bonamargy in a matter of four months in 1640.[23] But it was the outbreak of the 1641 Rebellion which eventually sealed the Mission's and Bonamargy's fate.

Patrick Heggarty who had been guardian of Bonamargy was arrested in Ballycastle, and the other Franciscans were now advanced in years and were worn out from their labours. The Mission was formally re-established in January 1647 but ended abruptly in June that year at the massacre of Dunaverty Castle. The celebrated Alexander Mac Colla Ciotach Mac Donnell (Colkitto) had fought with the Earl of Montrose in a campaign against Campbell and Convenanter forces. They were victorious in battle after battle until Philiphaugh where many of the Irish serving under Manus O'Cahan were killed. The wives of these men perished too, "many big with child, yet none of them were spared".[24]

Then at Dunaverty after the castle's surrender, the garrison were taken prisoner, manacled and butchered, many of them hurled from the cliffs.[25] Against this backdrop the Franciscan Mission ended, and Bonamargy itself appears to have been abandoned about then. The friary may then have been used for Anglican worship, as Ramoan church was under Presbyterian control for a period.[26] Alice Mac Donnell, Countess of Antrim had fled from her castle at Ballycastle during the 1641 Rebellion, to Tyrone and was accommodated with her O'Neill relations there. After the Restoration (1660) she returned to Ballycastle, hoping to regain her lands and property. In 1661 she was in residence at Bonamargy, two years later she was dead, and buried in Tyrone amongst her kin.[28]

A general chapter of the Franciscans held on 15th August 1687 resolved to create a new community at Bonamargy[29] proof positive that the friars had left by then. Since that date only burials have taken place in Bonamargy, the last occurred in January 1990. A wedding was celebrated in the friary in 2004, the first for almost three and a half centuries. The most common surname found on headstones in the adjoining graveyard is that of McCormick with a total of fifteen. Another local name, McNeill (with its various spellings) takes second place with thirteen headstones.

Benmore

Returning to Fair Head again there is an early ecclesiastical site called Killowen with a standing stone, and the site of a church and graveyard.[30] Griffith c1860 gives the extent of the graveyard as 20 perches.[31] There is a local tradition of a graveyard in the adjacent townland of Tirvillin, but at present there is no evidence of one. The Boyd estate at one time planned to erect a ditch from the Warren to Loughfadden which overlooks Murlough. All tenants north of the ditch were to be evicted and the enclosed land was to become a deerpark. Work is said to have begun in the 1840's, but for some reason the ditch was never completed. Traces of the ditch survive on Boyle's farm, Tornaroan, and also on the farm of the late Pat McBride, Ballyreagh.

When one of the Boyds came of age, the event was celebrated by a massive bonfire on the point of Fair Head. Fuel for the bonfire was provided by the tenants on the estate who were instructed to draw two cart loads of turf each. Those who resided furthest away from Fair Head spent two days in this unpaid capacity, nor were they paid for the turf.[32] Two centuries ago farmers paid a tax of one-tenth the value of their annual harvest. This tax which was called tithe was extremely unpopular, as it went directly to pay the upkeep of the Established church.

In some areas such as Culfeightrin parish the tithes were virtually impossible to collect. One example was when the tithes went unpaid and the churchwardens decided to act. When they "went to enforce the raising of money in lieu of tithe it was opposed and one of them, a particular friend of the vicar (Hill), narrowly escaped with his life." This occurred about the year 1796.[33] On the 1830's Ordnance Survey map a pound is shown at Twenty acres, opposite Dooey plantation. Formerly it was the practice to have stray animals impounded in a secure enclosure called a pound until a fee was paid for their release. There is a reference in 1814 to "Ballylicken Pound," which was along the old Ballycastle/Cushendall Road. Ballylicken is a mis-rendering of Ballyucan and it is likely that the pound at Twenty acres was referred to as "Ballyucan". Another possibility is that the facility at Twenty acres had been preceeded by an earlier one at Ballyucan.

By the time of Griffith's valuation the Twenty acres pound has been replaced by a new one at Ballyvoy. Margaret "McKeirnan" was the tenant of a house, twelve acres of land and the pound. This property was leased from John McGildowny, Clare Park, Ballycastle.[35] The pound was situated opposite Hunter's Bar, at a later date the fees were collected by McBride the local blacksmith.[36] There were once pounds at Ballycastle, Ballintoy, Rathlin, Loughguile, Dunluce, Falnaglass near Cushendall, Red Bay and elsewhere in north Antrim. Craigfad National School was not recorded by the Ordnance Survey Memoirs in July 1835, but it may have been one of the two schools which they omitted.[37] In Griffith's Valuation c1860 the school-house valued at ten shillings was leased from the representatives of Hugh Boyd. There was no schoolyard.[38] The school-house had a thatched roof which one night was ripped off in a storm sometime before 1901.

The school was then transferred to Colliers Row at Ballyreagh, where two houses were converted for the purpose. Despite the new location the school continued to be known as Craigfad National School, and at one time there were 70 pupils on the rolls.[39] Molly McCaughan, Gerard Ramsden and Sarah McGrath (grandmother of John and Jim McClements) are recalled as teachers at Craigfad. The old roofless school-house remained a ruin for many years before it was eventually demolished. A fireplace and a pair of ornamental pillars marking the entrance are all that has survived. The site is on the opposite side of the road from Jim and Betty McClement's farmhouse.[40]

The Cross and Passion College camogie team played a Carey team at Colliers Hall in February 1926, with the former winning twelve points to nil. Mr Ramsden, the Craid fad public elementary school teacher refereed the match. This was followed by the Craigfad school hurling team playing St. Kevin's, Ballycastle with the visitors running out winners six points to nil.[41] A school photo of 1931 shows 43 pupils, their teacher, Master Ramsden, with a son Padraig. Shortly afterwards the Ramsdens moved from the area and were last heard of in Andersonstown. Craid fad school closed in the1930s and its pupils were transferred to a new primary school at Barnish.[42]

Place-names

The late Pat McBride, Ballyreagh, a pupil at Craigfad, won first prize for his list of place-names in a school exam. The list is entirely local with some from Rathlin, and others are from Ramoan Parish. These I have deleted along with those which are townland names. Pat's spelling has been retained throughout. Unfortunately no precise locations are given and the place-names which follow all appear to be from the general Fair Head area. First on the list is Crockbrack (speckled hill) which is on Pat's farm.
Alt; Acha; Altadreen; Ballynamona; Buley; Bonavow; Brishe; Murlough; Bellahalliagh; Benmore (Fair Head) Carrickilbore; Crockofata; Crookancarragh, near Doonmore; Cravack; Craignagatt, S.McBride's farm, Cross; Crookaskre; Cree; Casnalough; Crook; Crookmore; Cloughabanes; Criskenbarrow; Drumaneal; Drimadonial; Doonbeg (this may be the Doonbeg on Rathlin).
Evish; Falmore; Fassinasillagh; Ferisky; Falcrose; Fyannachs, "a wee wet field on Seamus McBride's farm", Fargin Ard; Fargin Dubh (on cliff beyond Portnaloub) Fargin is understood here as a step; Ferlevia, "the Grey

Man used to go down here at the Grey Man's Path to fish."
Gortalorkin; Gortentober; Gobgurragh; Golocks; Kinareagh; Lacknakielt,
John Darragh's farm, Doonmore; Lacknakelly; Lakielk; Lackivea;
Lacknagran; Lackin; Lacknatry (Lack-na-traw, between Fair Head and
Murlough); Lignagunanagh; Ligahapple; Lough Fagin (Lough Fadden);
Lough Buye; Maghalouey; Merrich; Moniribbigh; Macknagarnan;
Skelefothey; Senvan (at Gortalorkin); Scrale Dubh; Slugin; Tirvirua;
Toberdoney, Darragh's farm; Ualareagh.

There is said to have been a battle fought at Lacknakielt but
nothing is known regarding the date or who the combatants were. Buley is
a swampy area of East of the old colliery houses and near a small
plantation on Crockbrack in Ballyreagh.[42]

Transhumance

Buley and Booly in placenames mean summer pasture (Gaelic
Buaile), a reminder of the ancient practice of transhumance. This was
where cattle were grazed during the summer months, herded by a group of
boys who lived in rough shelters. These shelters of stone and sods known
as booley houses were numerous on the higher ground of the Antrim hills.
There are booley house sites on Frank McCarry's land at Flughery and on
John Black's farm, Magheraboy in Knockbrack townland.[43]

Another booley site is on Seamus McBride's land on the shore of
Loughnacrannagh, approximately 200 yards East of the sheep dip.[44] A
group of six circular boley houses were discovered among whins on
Knocklayde above the Hanging Woods.[45] Other Glens sites are
Crocknaboley in Coolnagoppagh, Altnavooly at Tenaghs, Glenshesk,
Galboly near Garron Point and Ballyvooly, Cushendall. Professor Estyn
Evans states that it is significant that the Irish word for boy (buachaill)
originally meant a herdsman.[46] Anglicised as boghall, boghill and bohill this
pinpoints other possible booley sites. Crockannaboghal is in East Torr,
Cloughaboghill is in Lemnagh Beg, Ballintoy, and Curraghvohil near
Carnlough is a known booley site. At the latter location there are a number
of tan holes indicating that tanning occurred here.[47] Previously the
assumption was that the boys had passed their time playing games, but this
casts a whole new perspective on the subject.

On Knocklayde there are a number of small lime kilns, some of which pre-date the 1830s. Here is another occupation, lime quarrying and burning at which the young herders may have been employed. In some areas peat cutting may have been engaged in, however the herding of cattle was their main task. The cattle had to be kept away from cliffs or treacherous bogs and particular care taken in periods of mist or thick fog. Wolves were another threat, the last animal killed in Co. Antrim was said to be at Garron Point.[48] The practice of boleying survived until the 1930s on the slopes of Croaghaun at the Western end of Achill Island. Here, a group of teenagers at a height of almost 2,000 feet herded cattle and horses, but their future lay elsewhere.[49]

Another word found in placenames which can indicate a boleying site is cró which means cattle hut and is usually anglicised as "crow". Knocknacrow and Drumcrow in Glendun are two local examples, another is Evishnacrow. The latter is a known boley site, described as such by the Ordnance Survey Memoirs in the 1830s. Knocknacrow was pronounced Knocknacraw by an older generation and in Ballycastle cró was anglicized as crew and this was the word used for pigsties.[50] The Boley Fair held annually in Co. Down, and the Cork folk group the Boley Boys (1993) recall the practice of transhumance. Nomadic youths in the hills and marginal areas were replaced by the solitary shepherd in a purpose built herd's house.

Herds

Griffith records herd's houses in Carey and Glenshesk under the following townlands; Eglish, Ballynagard (2), Drumnakeel, Losset, Ballyvoy, Ballyreagh Upper, Bighouse, East Torr (2) West Torr, Ballyvennaght, Ballypatrick (2) Glenmakeeran, Tenaghs, Ardaghmore, Drumcullin, Ballyveely (2), Kilrobert (2), Tavnaghboy, Corvally and Ardagh (2). The last 8 are in Ramoan Parish and there are a further 17 in that parish; Carnsampson, Gortconny, Drummans (2), Capecastle, Carnately (2), Cloughanmurry (2), Magheramore, Moyarget Upper, Broommore (2), Broombeg, (2) Kilcreg and Town Parks.

Jamie McCart who lived at Glenmakeeran was one of the last herds. He married a McCormick, but the couple had no children. Jamie who herded to Alec Black collapsed and died at the end of his peat stack. There was a herd's house at Aghashimmer, Ballypatrick, Paddy Murphy and his family were the last to reside here. The house is now demolished and the area is a picnic site in Ballypatrick Forest. Johnny McAuley and Pat Mulholland were herds at Coolnagoppagh, the latter was known as Pat the Shepherd, his house is now wallsteads. The McMullan brothers, Paddy, Jamie and Tommy were all herds who lived at Coolnagoppagh. They and their sister Cissie were known as Roe. Paddy is said to be the Paddy Roe of the "Oul Lammas Fair" song, although this is disputed. Tommy Roe herded to Dan McBride, Watertop, his wife Mary Ann is recalled selling fowl in Ballycastle.[50] Thomas Mc"Mullen" is recorded by Griffith c1860 as a herd at Coolnagoppagh, but his house is not described as a herd's house. Yet John McCambridge, Jas. Shiel & Partners were described as Immediate Lessors of the house.[51]

Griffith gives the area attached to each herd's house, Drumacullin, Glenshesk, 1028 acres, landlord James S. Moore. At Ballypatrick the area was 1,140 acres and the tenants were John McCambridge and Archibald Butler, under the Earl of Antrim. Ardaghmore, 1442 acres, landlord, Arthur Devlin and at Glenmakeeran Thomas McCall is given as the occupier of 1902 acres. At both places the proprietor was the Earl of Antrim.[52] The McCollums of Tavnaghboy, Glenshesk were herds to McGildowny, Clare Park.[53] Archibald McCauley, Corvally, Glenshesk was a herd in 1872, and Wm McFall was a gamekeeper in 1874 at Glenmakeeran.

Daniel McCormick was a herd at Watertop in 1865. He may have been related to the McCormick family who were living 60 years later at Barard in Glenshesk. Previously a John Herrigan had lived at Barard, he was related to the McCluskeys, Loughguile.[54] Alec McCormick, senior was the last herd to live in the isolation of Barard. The family had a garden of potatoes, cabbage and turnips, fresh water was obtained from a small stream nearby, which froze in winter. When the Forestry Commission erected a fence here, many moor fowl were killed when they flew into the netting. Partridge were shot, hares snared and pheasants trapped, all providing fresh meat for the family. The house had one room with a South facing front door, a small kitchen and a zinc roof. Today only wallsteads remain with a massive fuchsia hedge blocking the doorway, and nettles and willowherb in the interior. Benweed grows from a wall and conifers encroach from all sides, soon nature will have reclaimed everything. There were plants growing at Barard known as "wolf fire" which lit up when one pressed upon them.[55] I have yet to locate and identify these plants, they may now be extinct due to the aforestation of the area.

Archie Duffin herded sheep at Fair Head, and later worked to Neil Dallat, Ballycastle. The Duffins lives at Colliers Row, and also in one of the old colliery houses at Crockbrack, they were the last to live here.[56] Greer Hamilton & Gailey, Ballymoney hold a list of the tenants of Colliers Row dated 26th October 1907; John Dillon, James Delargy, Arthur Stewart*, John McFaul, John Clarke, John Fyfe, John Blaney, John Dixon, James Murray and A. McGonigal.

Arthur Stewart* was a miner at Ballyreagh mine, later he worked in Ballycastle and lived in a cottage at The Chaster, Drumawillan. A son Willie who was born at Colliers Row also worked in the mines but later worked for different farmers.the North Antrim Mining Syndicate in Spring 1905 began boring operations at Ballyreagh where they discovered a fine foot seam of coal at a depth of 250 feet. They then sank two shafts, one to work the coal, the other was a ventilating shaft, with a connecting gallery. Accidents in the mines were an almost daily occurrence, the following report is from October 1905. Although no location is given the incident may have been at Ballyreagh.

Peculiar Ballycastle Accident

*An accident occurred yesterday at Ballycastle coal mines, which fortunately is not serious but might easily have had fatal results. The engineer was down the shaft inspecting and directing some operations. At the completion of same the dinner hour had arrived, and the man in charge of the steam lift had gone for his meal. Not aware of this, the engineer signalled to be hoisted up and another man undertook the duty and turned on steam. When the shift came to the top the man at the engine could not turn off steam and the bucket continued to ascend into the air. Another man was along with the engineer in the bucket and he, seeing the position of matters, jumped out and sustained scarcely any injury. The bucket was stopped by the beam, to which it was suspended, and the engineer sustained a severe crushing, some of his ribs being broken. Dr. McIlroy, JP, was at once in attendance and the injured man carefully looked after and conveyed to his residence where he is doing well.
24/10/1905.*

In July 1906 a private company The Belfast Coal and Iron Limited was formed and they acquired the mineral rights over an area of 1,000 acres.

BELFAST TELEPHONE Nº
BALLYCASTLE TELEPHONE Nº
ADDRESSES:
SOUTH HILL, BALLYCASTLE,
Co. ANTRIM, IRELAND,
AND
60, ANN STREET, BELFAST.

SOUTH HILL,
BALLYCASTLE,

TELEGRAPHIC ADDRESSES
"BRIQUETTE, BELFAST.
"BRIQUETTE, BALLYCAS
Cº ANT

21st Decr. 1906.

PLEASE ADDRESS ALL COMMUNICATION
TO THE COMPANY

BELFAST COAL AND IRON LIMTED.

PROPRIETORS OF THE BALLYCASTLE COAL AND IRON MINES.

ALL QUOTATIONS AND SALES ARE SUBJEC. TO USUAL STRIKE AND STOPPAGE CLAUSE
AND TO ACCEPTANCE BY RETURN OF POST, UNLESS OTHERWISE SPECIFIED

B.C.& I. Ltd. Letterhead

The platform for the wheels and the lifting gear were made and erected by Neal and Peter Dallat, Ballycastle. During the sinking of the shafts the workmen encountered a sixteen foot seam of clay. When analysed later the clay was discovered to be suitable for the production of fire bricks and other fire-clay products. B.C. & I. Ltd. immediately commenced erecting machinery, kilns, drying sheds and a 150 foot chimney, all from their own brick.[58]

Brick, B.C.& I. Ltd, from Ballyreagh, photograph by Hugh McGill

132

The manager was a Scot named Brodie, believed by some locals to be Belgian, who lived on the Quay Road, Ballycastle. He emigrated it is said to South Africa when production at Ballyreagh ceased (the North Antrim Standard, 15/4/1909 reported that he was not then in Ballycastle). Only a few of the locals who worked at Ballyreagh are recalled now, Hugh Dillon, who was involved in the boring, John Murphy, James McKinley and a McDonnell of Dunacalter who was a clerk. Local farmers were quick to invest capital in the new venture, but the gamble failed,[59] despite all the early promising reports.

A ton of cannel coal from Ballyreagh was made into gas – great excitement prevailed – their output at present is 150 – 200 tons of coal weekly. B.C.& I. Ltd are erecting blast furnaces at their pits for the production of pig-iron from their seam of ironstone. April 1907; the price for fire-bricks is £4-12-0 per 1,000 in Belfast and their plant capable of manufacturing 80,000 fire-bricks per week is on the verge of being completed.[60] Coal sold at £1 per ton in February 1908 and unscreened coal at nineteen shillings (95p) delivered in Ballycastle. At the same period their building brick were sold on site at twenty six shillings (£1.30) per 1,000.[61] Sole agents for the Belfast Coal & Iron Limited were the Dublin Fireclay Company Limited with a registered office at 15 College Square.

The company's factory at 77 Sir Rogerson's Quay planned to manufacture a wide range of sanitary pipes, flue liners, gas retorts, cupolas, boiler seatings, blue bricks, tiles, fire bricks, silica bricks etc.[62] This letter was dated 10th March 1908 but soon afterwards B.C.& I. Ltd ceased production, in July 1908 all their plant and machinery at Ballyreagh was sold off.[62] One reason given for the closure was that the bricks were said to be under burnt, thus exposing them to frost damage.[63] But an examination of the bricks remaining on site does not reveal any such damage after almost ninety years.

Each brick is inscribed B.C. & I. Ltd., and below the letters there is a small pick. Ballyreagh was only one of a number of places in the Ballycastle area where bricks were manufactured over the previous two centuries. Locations included Carvacloughan (between Moyarget and the Dry Arch), on Todds farm, Drumawillan, Ballycastle, and along the R. Tow in Townparks. Another reason given for the closure was that the mine had great potential with an estimated 55 million tons of coal available. As a result an English firm took over the mine and closed it apparently to prevent competition with English mines.[64]

Craigfad Mine

The name means long rock and the mine is on the farm of Johnny Butler and adjacent to the children's graveyard at Killaleenan. The Scottish firm Merry and Cunningham worked the Craigfad mine c1860 (but it is not recorded in Griffith's Valuation). In 1920 John Reid leased the mine which had a four foot seam (Main Coal) supported by a sandstone roof. He began clearing away the accumulated debris until a basalt dyke was reached. A shaft was then sunk beyond the dyke and coal was discovered nearer the surface. This was good quality coal which sold at £3.00 (£3.15) per ton in Ballycastle , June 1920, cartage was included. Then a new dyke was encountered at right angles to the first, but no coal was found beyond this dyke. Reid subsequently surrendered the mine which was then leased by a Mr Parland of Coalisland in February 1922, but after a few months exploratory work he too abandoned the workings.[65] The mine finally closed in 1967 and one local paper reported on the closure;

Ballycastle coal mine – one of Europe's oldest – ends.

THE COAL MINE at Ballycastle – one of the oldest in Europe – has been closed down.

Lord Antrim, owner of Ballycastle Mines Ltd. Which worked the pit for the past 10 years, said today – "We have come to the end of the seam of coal. The mine is no longer profitable to work." The equipment used at the mine will be sold at an auction later this month. About 10 miners were employed and five of these were paid off two months ago. The steady supply of coal from the mine ceased some time ago.

For hundreds of years the Ballycastle coal served domestic and industrial interests and because it was mined locally was cheaper than imported fuel. Some people considered the coal burned too quickly and that was why it was sold cheaply, but the Lord Antrim disagreed. He commented: "The coal was of good quality."[66]

Jimmy McVeigh, Acravally worked as a miner for 5 years at Craigfad, having previously worked for about 5 years in a mine near Doncaster. These are his recollections of Craigfad; The mine entrance sloped steeply, the coal was hauled out in bogies and there was constant dripping from the roof of the mine. A short distance from the entrance there was an airshaft, 33 feet in depth. The men worked a 5½ day week from eight to five and to midday on Saturdays.

The miners were Jamie Butler, Craigfad, Hughie McNeill, Ballyvoy, Paddy Brown, Glenshesk, Mick McAuley, Ned Hill, John Butler, Archie McCormick, Dan Rankin, John Murphy and Bill Mayne. Alex McKinney, Capecastle was a coal merchant who came on a daily basis to purchase coal at Craigfad. With his lorry loadened Alex then made deliveries to his regular customers in the Ballycastle area.[67] Bill Mayne (foreman at Craigfad) was a Scot who arrived in Ballycastle on a 6 month contract. He had previously worked in South Africa and in the Drumlemble coalfield between Machrihanish and Campbeltown. Bill who lived at Atlantic Avenue, Ballycastle named his house "Craigfad."[68]

John G. Loughran visited Craigfad a short time after it had closed and wrote a fascinating account of what he observed. "There are several corrugated iron huts, all in fairly good condition but the tall pine poles that supported the loading shed have already begun to sag and decay. The wind whistles through the sheltered windows and rattles a loose door. There are rags and broken tools and timber rotting in pools of grey water." There is an interview with 74 year old Bob Butler, Ballyvoy who had been a miner for 25 years. "It's a hard dirty life but once you've started you're like a sailor – you don't want to work at anything else." Bob suffered from bronchitis and had lost his sight, yet if he had to do it all over again he would still choose mining.[69]

Blackpark Mine, above Ballyvoy was opened in 1950 when James Delargy sunk a shaft. The miners and bogies were all lifted and lowered by means of a winch. Jamie Davidson who was transferred from Murlough recalled the constant dripping of water which caused him to leave after a year or so. James O'Brien and Harry O'Mullan were two miners transferred from Murlough, they lived in a house of Paddy McCambridge's and travelled home at weekends. Local men who worked at Blackpark included Pat McAuley, The Warren, Pat McBride, Ballyvoy, Jamie Butler and his brother "Wee" Bob, the Rankin brothers, and 'Big" Paddy McGowan, Armoy Glen. Jim Smith was mine engineer, and after the mine's closure he went to live in a village near Hamilton in Scotland.

Jamie Davidson manned the pumps at Blackpark, which was worked in two shifts, his take-home pay was £4-10-0 (£4.50).[70] Water in the mine was drained away through an old bore hole, which became blocked on occasions. On one occasion dynamite was used to clear the blockage.[71] Blackpark had closed by 1961 as Craigfad was then the only mine in operation.[72] At Drumahitt there is said to be a great seam of coal at a depth of 80 feet, which was never worked.[72] Griffith records a series of bores drilled in the area in 1816, which included "Drumah" (Drumahitt).

Other locations were along the Carey River beyond the mill (October 1816) and at Barnish, South of "Muckmine." Three quarters of a mile SE of the latter and close to the North side of the road to "Cushendaal" was another. At Eglish, close to the river a bore was sunk 31 yards, 2 feet. Four coal seams were passed through, the first was 1 foot 5 inches thick. A tradition prevailing at Eglish in 1816 was that coal had formerly been discovered and worked here. The final bore was made at Drumadoon, January 11th 1817. These trials were made by Mr Brough who was described as "an experienced English Coal Miner."[73] Coal and turf were the main fuel in use when the mines closed, but in less that half a century oil and electricity have replaced them. The same period has seen numerous other changes including the demise of the local blacksmith.

Blacksmiths

The McBrides forge at Ballyvoy was established about 1902, in the former pound across the road from Hunters Bar. Customers brought along a quantity of turf and if there were three at the one time then this saved on the fuel (for the smith). Harrows were made for the firm of John McElderry, Ballymoney whose van collected the implements on a regular basis. Link chains were also made in the smithy which closed in1954. Jim McBride was a fiddler whose repertoire included "The Lark in the Clear Air." He was recorded playing his tune c1918, perhaps by the late Sam Henry, Coleraine,[74] (who is known to have visited the forge at a later date).

Jamie Davidson recalled his neighbour Charlie McCloskey, Drumnakeel, making cartwheels which were shod in the McBride's forge. Three wheel rims were made at a time using a fire of turf. Jamie was a youngster at the time and he helped stoke the fire which took two hours to reach the required temperature. When conditions were right the McBrides lifted the hoop with tongs on to the cartwheel and hammered both into position. Old Jamie McBride the blacksmith had two sons Jim and Paddy who were also smiths. They were assisted by a relation from near Ballinlea, Felix McGonigle who died single.

The men often worked late at night and local youngsters often congregated there. The men made a wide range of implements including drill ploughs, wheels for donkey carts, tongs, hinges, latches, hearth bars and gaffs were made from old pitch forks. Turf spades were made, sometimes using the mould board of an old drill plough. Three legged pots which were cracked or had a small hole were patched with a small plate of iron over the damaged area. During World War Two when heels for hob nailed boots were hard to obtain, Waxey Butler was kept supplied by the Ballyvoy forge.[75]

In 1815 there is a reference to "Robert McBride's smith shop" which was near Alex Ranken's house and in the vicinity of the mines.[76] This was one of at least 5 forges which were located near the mines at different dates. The others were at the White Mine, the West Mine, Colliery Port and Carrickmore. Another forge was located at Dan McVeigh's house in Broughanlea. A family called Hutchinson previously lived here and earlier there were the McMullans who were blacksmiths. A child was scalded to death in this house but it's name has now been forgotten.[77]

Patrick McMullen had a house and forge at Drumadoon c1860, leased from John Darragh, the annual valuation of both buildings was ten shillings (50p).[78] John Dillon had a forge with an annual valuation of ten shillings leased from Robert Sharpe,at Drumnakeel c1860.[79] A reference is made to the old smith's shop at Drumnakeel in 1899,[80] where there is a field called the Smith's Shop Field. Along the lane here is a flat rock with embedded irons which the smiths used.[81] A blacksmith nicknamed "Bishop" who lived at Blackpark worked at the Drumnakeel forge.[82] The "Bishop's" farm was later owned by Neal Dallat and is presently owned by the Huggins family.[83]

A Robert McHenry, blacksmith, Farrenmacallan, had a son Henry, blacksmith who married in 1867. There was formerly a smithy at Altnacartha in Cushleake but by the 1850's it had been abandoned.[84] The Camerons were Ballycastle blacksmiths who came from the Cushleake area.[85] They later moved to Ballyshannon and finally emigrated to Canada and the United States. The Camerons were related to two other blacksmith families, the McLaughlins and Russells.[86]

Glenshesk appears to have had few forges, one was located at Greenans on the left of the lane down to McBrides. A portion of the smithy walls and the hoop used in making the cart wheels were still to be seen a few years ago. This lane was known locally as the Lough Road as it led to a small lough now drained called Loughangorm. There was at one time a particular design of gate which was known as the Glenshesk gate. The design consisted of five horizontal bars with an upright in the centre of the gate. In addition there was a semi circular bar which curved from the bottom right hand corner to the top bar and down to the other corner. One of the last known examples of the Glenshesk gate is on the farm of Billy Boylan at Greenans.[87]

Butchers

The pig butcher is another vanished trade, the last butcher in Carey was Jamie Davidson, Drumnakeel who died in 2004. He learned the trade from his father Tom who had once worked with Jack McFadden whose family had a shop at Malladeevan. It was Jack who had taught Tom how to kill sheep. Jamie killed pigs on 119 farms in Carey and Glenshesk, from Torr to Ardagh. He also butchered outside this area killing seven pigs one morning for Alex Christie, Craiganee, 4 miles from Ballycastle. When Jamie began the work in the late 1920's, payment was one shilling per animal and the task could take from twenty to thirty minutes. Once though Jamie claims to have killed 4 pigs in an hour which was considered to be "good going".

The most important aspect of pig butchering was the temperature of the water which had to be "tempered". This was done by first boiling the water and then adding the correct amount of cold water. Pig butchers carried up to six knives in a leather scabbard, and every Monday night Jamie carefully greased his tools with olive oil. This was done in order to keep the knives in good condition which was essential. When the knives needed sharpening Jamie made the short journey to Drumnakeel Bridge where the sandstone coping served as his personal grindstone.

The Davidsons kept a boar at Drumnakeel for many years and local farmers were charged four shillings (20p) to have their sows serviced. The Ministry of Agriculture supplied the boar, which they replaced every three year. Joe McConaghy of Mullarts in Glenshesk brought a sow to the Davidsons one time. Before he left Joe plucked a bunch of nettles and he proceeded to make the sign of the cross at the sow's tail. As Jamie had never seen nor heard of this practice before he asked what this was all about. McConaghy replied that this was to ensure a good litter of pigs. But Jamie saw that the sow had been stung and he was not impressed by this old freet. The pig butcher looked upon this as nothing more than animal cruelty.

Another recollection was the day Denis Cassley senior of Doonfin arrived with horse and cart to have his sow serviced. On arrival at Drumnakeel the cart was discovered to be empty – the sow had somehow escaped undetected from the open cart. A search was begun for the missing animal and Jamie accompanied the farmer as he journeyed back up the glen. At the Big Bridge they found the sow safe and well, fast asleep by the roadside. Once when Jamie went to kill two pigs for a Carey woman called Mary Ann he asked her for hot water. The woman then lit a fire with paper bags but instead of adding peats she added more paper bags. This method took a long time to boil the water and Jamie was infuriated at his time being wasted in such a manner.

The shoulders of boars were known as boars saddles and these had at an earlier period been used as saddles.[88] After pigs were killed they were skinned by scraping the hair off using a sharp knife but some poorer families dispensed with the services of a pig butcher and killed the animal themselves. On occasions the hair of the pig was scraped off with a sharpened tin lid![89] Alex McCollum, Drumnakeel was a pig butcher, his family has previously lived at Ballypatrick where they are remembered by the placename McCollum's Brae. Although they were not behind with their rent, the McCollums were evicted from their Ballypatrick holding. Another local pig butcher was Hugh McCormick who was known as The Buffer, he lived in Glenshesk at the foot of Cool Brae. Mickie McMullan who was from "over the mountain" established a butchers shop at Collier's Row and here he did his slaughtering. Mickie "Mutton" as he was called had a dray and he travelled around selling meat from a basket.[90]

Stonemasons

Big Jamie McKinley, Lisnacalliagh, an uncle of the late Andy McKinley, Ballycastle was a stonemason and he was also a good musician. He regularly played his melodion at a ceilidh in Jeanie McNeill's house at Fair Head. Jamie also worked for a period in the Scottish coalmines but he is not known to have worked in the local mines. Jamie worked on many jobs with Alex McKinley (Andy's grandfather). The men carried out remedial work on the Margy and other bridges where they began by damming the river and making their own hoists. They often left home at 4.30 in the morning in a horse and cart to travel to their place of work.

Dan McKinley obtained the contract to construct the Quay Road footpath on the North side – the South side was completed by a different contractor. The McKinleys also repaired the roadside wall where it had been damaged by heavy seas in the Maguires Strand area. Hugh Hill, Clare Street, Henry Norton, Paddy McIlroy and a man named McGuile worked to Dan McKinley at various periods. McGuile was known only as Tarry, from his constant work tarring roads.[91] Cornelius Boyle was a farmer and a stonemason of Tornaroan who was recalled carrying out work at the Ballycastle Poorhouse. Dick Duffin, father of the late Dickie Duffin attended him on some contracts.[92] Barny Boyle was a Ballycastle stonemason who built a number of houses on Ann Street, and also the 4 houses called Bleachgreen Avenue. He also worked on the construction of the original Marine Hotel in the 1890's.[93]

McMichael Family

James McMichael, Churchfield was a fine mason credited with the construction of Ballyveridagh School in 1836-7.[94] He was related to the Ballycastle McMichaels who once had a pharmacy in Ann Street, and also a lease of the Royal Hotel. The McCanns who farmed at Acravally were also related to James and a field at Magheratemple is yet known as McMichael's field.[95] A Robert McMichael is recorded repairing roads around Carey in the early 1800s.[96] The 4 McMichael headstones in Bonamargy provide little information with the exception of the earliest stone dated 1714. Although the inscription is illegible now it was recorded over a century ago by Francis Joseph Bigger.[97]

HERE LYETH THE BODY OF
MARY McMICHAEL WHO DIED
AUGUST THE 14TH 1714 AGED —
NEAL McMICHAEL DIED MARCH
THE 16TH 1757. ALSO JOHN Mc
MICHAEL DIED MARCH THE
15 1753 AND MARY McMICHA
EL DIED OCTOBER THE 27
1755 CHILDREN TO DOUGAL
McMICHAEL OF EKERVELEY*
WHOSE AGE WAS 54 YEARS
*ACRAVALLY

The 1734 Census Records 4 "McMichiel" families in Ramoan Parish at Clare, Carnately and Toberbilly, with 2 in Culfeightrin, both at Barnish.[98] The first McMichael residence at Straid in Ballintoy Parish was a herd's house, today Tessie McMichael's residence is on the same site. This family state that they are related to the McMichaels of Carey and Ballycastle.[99] McMichael the Ballycastle undertaker was of different stock, his family had long been located at Novally near Ballycastle.[100] Yet another McMichael family were those of Craigbane, Glenshesk who had originated in Loughguile.[101]

Masons

James Stewart (1854-1950) Benvan, was a farmer, fisherman, stonemason and he was widely known as a herbalist.[102] The Lynn brothers Bob and Paddy of Ballyvoy were stonemasons, both worked on the constructions of Corrymeela.[103] Two other 20th century masons were Hugh Neill, Losset who settled at Glenstaghy, Ballintoy and Willie Gillan who moved to Magherahoney.[104] In the 1860s there were John McLaughlin, Ballyvoy, James McMullan and his son James, Drumnakeel and Matthew Neely, Drumahitt. The Neely family have now died out, they once had a shop in Ann Street, Ballycastle. Michael McGowan was a stonemason residing at Calhame in the 1870s.

Quarries

The stone used by the stonemasons came from various sandstone and blackstone quarries. The latter was the local name for basalt and one such quarry was located on Hunter's farm at Cross. Another blackstone quarry on Butlers farm at Craigfad supplied the stone used in the constructions of Drunmakeel Cottages, c1900. This quarry closed a few years later, as vernacular housing made increasing use of brick at the expense of stone. The Lough quarry was so named because of its location near Loughareema (the Vanishing Lake). "West of the lough at the Lough Brae" was the direction that I was given.

A stone breaker was in use at this quarry which supplied "spalls" for field drainage, road making and house foundations. Denis McKinley, Ballypatrick and John "Shannon" McNeill of the Top of the Water both worked here. Jamie Davidson recalled 2 days which he spent drawing stone from the quarry for a local farmer in the 1920s. He drew 3 loads per day and his pay was 3 shillings (15p) for the 2 days. At a later date Pat McMullan drew stone by lorry from the quarry for Antrim County Council. At Carrickaneigh near the old shooting lodge (now demolished) in Glenmakeeran there was a limestone quarry. Two men who worked here were Alex "Mick" McCormick, Drumnakeel and Dan Black, Coolnagoppagh who married a Rathlin woman named Kelly.

The limestone was burnt in kilns and the resulting lime was then spread by farmers on their fields to enhance their crop yields. The burning of the limestone was carried out without the use of coal, turf was the only fuel used. There were a large number of kilns in Carey a century ago with one on most of the larger farms. The McGills of Glenmakeeran had 2 kilns, one was built about 80 years ago, [105] a late date for the erection of such a structure. The history of the limestone quarries and especially the small kilns has gone largely unrecorded.

Clarke Family

Eneas Clarke had a farm at Acravally but was evicted, afterwards going to live at Coolnaoopagh where he was recorded c1861. He died at Broughanlea 19th March 1875 aged 68 and was buried in Carey. James, son of Eneas and the grandfather of the late Seamus Clarke became a cooper in Ballycastle. James married Margaret McLaughlin, Drumaroan, he died 28th June 1908 aged 68 and Margaret died 9th April 1912, both were buried in Carey.

Daniel, a brother of James was a carpenter who carried out work on the 2 houses called "Strandview", at North Street, Ballycastle. Later Daniel lived in one of the houses, he died 21ˢᵗ June 1886 from an injury caused by a rusty nail. This injury was either not properly treated or was not promptly treated, and Daniel died at the comparatively young age of 48. He was buried with his brother James in the same plot as their parents. James and Daniel had at least 2 sisters, one settled in Belfast and the other emigrated to the United States. John was another brother, he married Ellen Cassidy, 29ᵗʰ August 1866 in Ballycastle. The couple lived at Leyland, Whitehall and Carnsampson, a son Daniel born in 1876, died in 1884. John and Ellen's eldest son John served his time as a barman in Belfast and eventually became the proprietor of the Antrim Arms Hotel, Glenarm. He began writing under his pen-name "Benmore" and submitted articles to newspapers such as the Irish News, Irish Weekly, Derry People, Gaelic American and the Frontier Sentinel.

The latter was a Newry based paper which ceased printing in 1972. Benmore was a contributor to a local paper The Glensman during its brief life, and he often gave talks on historical and sporting themes. He was prominent in the establishment of the G.A.A. in Belfast and the Glens especially Glenarm where the local camogie club was named Benmore in his honour. Benmore was also an Irish language activist, archaeologist, antiquarian and an artist sketching scenes such as Bonamargy, Bengore, Glendun Viaduct, Glenariff and Slemish. A number of these were published by An Tuirne Beag, Ballycastle as postcards prior to the Great War. In "Thoughts From the Heart," published in 1908, Benmore writes of William Orr, Thomas Davis, Monsignor O'Laverty, Shane O'Neill, Rev R. Lyttle, Dungivey Abbey and other subjects.

"St. Brigid's Abbey", written in 1925 is an account of the establishment of the boarding school and convent in Ballycastle by the Cross and Passion sisters. This volume was followed two years later by "Memorials of John Hogan", a tribute to a forgotten Irish sculptor who died in 1857. He also wrote "A Short Life of Saint Brigid",[106] and a collection of his poems appeared under the title "Blossoms from the Hedgerows". The volume includes, "Rachery Isle", "Wintry-Winds", "On The Cave Hill, Belfast", "The Giant's Head, Antrim Coast", "The Dawn", "In Boyhoods Day near Ballycastle" and "The Star".

The headland which inspired his pen-name is commemorated in "Benmore, Co. Antrim". By 1934 Benmore was in failing health and he was admitted to Larne Hospital, where he died 24th May 1934. He was buried in his native Carey, in the same plot as his wife Isabella (nee Campbell) who died 22nd March 1923. Seamus Clarke, son of James, also became a cooper, later he emigrated to San Francisco where he continued his trade in a winery. He served as secretary of the Coopers Union in California and he became the champion cooper in California. For many years Seamus kept up correspondence with his old friends the Mooney family who were boot and shoemakers at Castle Street, Ballycastle.

John Clarke was Seamus' brother and he too became a cooper, having served his apprenticeship to his father. The Clarkes used rushes to seal the base of barrels and when completed the barrels were filled with sacks which were then sprinkled with water. This was done in order to keep the wood damp and therefore water tight. The main hoop in a barrel was known as the master hoop. Coopers who travelled around carrying out casual work were referred to as journeymen coopers. They carried a small anvil among their tools which were used for the making of small hoops. John Clarke once worked in oak which was imported from Liverpool and also Oregon pine but eventually the wood became too expensive. When a customer brought in an item for repair, John could tell at a glance which cooper had made the object.

Alex Watson, Ballycastle served his apprenticeship with the Clarkes, he later worked in the Avoniel Distillery, Belfast. John Jennings a native of Co. Down also served his time here and was later self employed with his workshop in the Market Yard.[108] John the Weigh-master in the yard died comparatively young. He was the grandfather of the late Sean Jennings.[109] John Clarke was the last cooper to practice his trade in Ballycastle, his workshop was at the rear of O'Connor's Bar, Ann Street. About 1920 John and his family moved to the Castle Bar and in one of the out-houses he established a workshop. Old residents recalled seeing the cooper's wares displayed along the footpath at the front of the public house. Then after 17 years, John and his wife Anne (nee Kenny) returned to their former residence in Ann Street.

Anne Kenny was a Co. Sligo woman who came to Ballycastle having obtained an offer of employment in the Antrim Arms Hotel. She died 7th May 1949 aged 76 and John died 11th February 1951. The couple left 3 children, Mary who was mainly involved in managing the bar, Annie who married John McKenna, Gortconny and James better known as Seamus. Mary died single in February 1974 aged 63, Annie died July 1988 aged 71 and her husband John died September 1993 aged 72.

Seamus worked in the bar and served for a period as local councillor but his main interests lay elsewhere. He had a passionate interest in local history and poetry and since his teens was involved with the local McQuillans Club. He also had a long association with the Glen Feis and the Roger Casement Commemoration Committee. Following the long tradition of the family Seamus became a writer in 1977. He wrote a 66 page booklet on Casement and the Irish language. A history of the Feis entitled "Feis na n Gleann" appeared in 1995 and he also compiled an anthology of poetry relating to the Feis. This little volume entitled "The Poetry of Feis na nGleann" contains verse by Louis J. Walsh, Benmore, Roger Casement, Cathal O'Byrne, William McDade and others. The latter poet who lived in Belfast had Drumavoley connections and may have lived there as a boy.[110] John Clarke (1888-1960) the potato breeder was related to Seamus Clarke's family[111] and the Clarkes of Breen, Drumnakeel and Portrush were all related.[112] Seamus, the last of his name died in March 2006 aged 91, he was interred in the same plot as his parents.

Cobblers

A Henry Butler of Ballyreagh was recorded as a shoemaker in 1870. Alex Butler, the son of "Wee" Bob Butler, Ballyvoy, became a cobbler and had a workshop opposite the car park at Hunter's Bar. This was a popular venue for card playing at night, one regular here was Jamie Davidson, Drumnakeel.[113] Later Waxey as he was known worked from premises in Ann Street, Ballycastle where Bobby Bell's shop is today. Alex lived nearby in Bleachgreen Avenue until the row was condemned, he then moved to Mayo Drive where he ended his days. Waxey also repaired shoes in Cushendall for a period, travelling there by motorbike. Mick McAuley, senior worked to him at this time and Dickie Duffin also worked to Waxey for some time.[114]

The Butlers have been resident in Carey since at least 1734 when they numbered 5 households in the census of that year; John Butler, Drumadoon, Peter Butler, Ballyucan, Richard, Coolnagoppagh, Robert and John Butler, both Tornaroan.[115] Butler is a Norman name and a possible origin of the Carey family is a "William McButlerogh" of Glenarm Parish, recorded in 1669.[116] That is assuming that the surname represents McButler Óg. Paddy, son of Dan Laverty, Greenans, Glenshesk was a cobbler who worked to Alex Butler. During World War Two Fisty as he was known made large numbers of shillelaghs which he sold to American soldiers stationed in the area. Big Andy McKinley did the painting of the shillelaghs. Dan Laverty died in the Dalriada Hospital in November 1987, he was aged over ninety.[117]

Laverty Family

The Lavertys have been resident in Carey and Glenshesk since at least the mid 17th century. The Hearth Money Rolls of 1669 record Laghlin O Leverty and Brian O Leverty at Ballypatrick. Edmond O Leverty was recorded in Glenshesk with 2 hearths (few houses had 2 hearths) and at Broombeg there was a Widd Laverty.[118] There are in Bonamargy two adjacent Laverty headstones situated close to the North gate of the little stone gatelodge. One, a large sandstone slab now flat has in each of the top corners a carved angel with inlaid lettering. The inscription is now weathered and is not easily deciphered;

OWEN LAVERTY
Of Ballycastle in memory of his
father Owen who departed this
life AD 1836 Aged 82 years
And his brother Patrick 30th
Oct. 1815 Aged 22 years
Also his son Daniel, 7th June 1816,
Aged three years.
Likewise his son James 3rd
Sep. 1818 Aged 10 days
Owen Laverty of BC. Died
23rd May 1851 aged 32 years
Also his wife Mary who died
29th Dec. 1851 aged 32 years

The adjacent stone appears to have had something broken off the top section, perhaps a small sandstone cross. The inscription reads;

SACRED
TO THE MEMORY OF
JAMES LAVERTY
BALLYCASTLE
DIED 8TH APRIL 1871
AGED 50 YEARS
AND
ANNIE
HIS DAUGHTER
DIED 20TH DECEMBER 1867
AGED 12 YEARS
May they rest in peace

This family were involved in the licensed trade of Ballycastle for some decades, Mrs Owen Laverty was a publican of Main Street in 1843.[119] James Laverty was proprietor of the Royal Hotel in 1848 when he advertised in the local paper.[120] Although James was buried in Bonamargy, his wife Catherine was buried at St. Patrick & St. Brigid's, Ballycastle. A third Laverty headstone at Bonamargy lies within the walls of the friary. Almost illegible now it is to an Eneas Laverty who died in October 1771? Aged 55. He may be related to the Eneas Laverty who was farming at Drumeeny in the 1830s. Hugh Laverty in 1838 was a teacher at Brackney, the school was held in an outhouse and had 30 pupils on the rolls.[121]

Two Laverty households at Greenans, Glenshesk are recorded by Griffiths Valuation as Lafferty, which is a Donegal spelling of the name.[122]

The blacksmiths, coopers, miners, pig butchers, shoemakers, stonemasons, thatchers and all the old trades were swept aside as the 20th Century gathered momentum. The tradesmen and unskilled workers toiled hard – then they were gone. Many of them left no memorial in their work, nor a photograph of their image. Their lives had passed as if they were a mirage, like the Fata Morgana which had been observed on occasions off the North Coast. A 12 year old girl, and other witnesses observed the phenomenon once near Sheep Island. They saw rows of white washed houses, green fields and tall hedges, out over the water, then suddenly all vanished.[123] The mirage was seen by people in Carey who stored it in their folk memory.

The last word goes to the late Jamie McKiernan, Ballycastle, who was a natural story teller. Jamie was reared at Tornaroan and had heard his neighbours talk of the enchanted green island which appeared off the Pans Rocks. One very warm summer the enchanted island appeared, its trees shimmered in a heat haze for some time – then it was gone.

References, Chapter Three

1.   Ulster Journal of Archaeology, Third Series, 1938. pp 122-135
2.   McCahan's Local Histories
3.   Mac Gabhann, p149
4.   Forgotten Places of the North Coast, p129. Clegnagh Publishing. Revised Edition 1991
5.   Pat McBride (deceased)
6.   Elizabeth & Joe Martin, Cloughmills
7.   Pat McBride (deceased)
8.   O'Laverty Vol 4, p486
9.   Griffith Valuation, p54
10.   Griffith Valuation, p52
11.   John Duncan, Drumnakeel
12.   Jamie Davidson
13.   Dickie Duffin
14.   D.E. brochure 1977
15.   Glynns Vol15, pp 34,35
16.   Coleraine Tribune p26, 5/6/1985, A Glensman's Diary by Cahal Dallat J.P.
17.   O'Laverty Vol4, p343
18.   Coleraine Tribune, 5/6/1985
19.   Jim McCormick, Rathmoyle, formerly Leyland Road
20.   O.S. Memoirs Vol 24, p64
21.   Macdonnells of Antrim, p220
22.   Glynns Vol16, pp 33-38
23.   Glynns Vol 7 P8
24.   Glynns Vol 14, p41
25.   Macdonnells of Antrim, p107
26.   Glynns Vol 6, p7
27.   Macdonnells of Antrim, p437
28.   Bun-na-Margie, p38. Francis Joseph Bigger M.R.I.A, F.R.S.A. Belfast 1898
29.   O'Laverty Vol4, p471
30.   Seamus McBride, Cross
31.   Ballycastle Union, p54
32.   Pat McBride (deceased) Ballyreagh
33.   Hugh A. Boyd, quoting from Dalriada Parishes
34.   Grand Jury Presentation Book for County Antrim, Summer Assizes, 1814, p28

35. Ballycastle Union, p55
36. Pat McBride (deceased)
37. Glynns 5, p56
38. Ballycastle Union, p53
39. Pat McBride
40. John McClements, Drumeeny
41. Irish News, 25/2/1998
42. Pat McBride
43. Pat Denis
44. Pat McBride
45. David Dillon
46. Irish Folk Ways, p27. Professor E.E.Evans
47. Glynns Vol 4, p30
48. Joe Shiels (deceased) Moyarget
49. Glynns Vol 6, p25
50. Jamie Davidson
51. Ballycastle Union p47
52. Ballycastle Union pp45,46,50
53. Randal McDonnell, Glenshesk
54. John McClements
55. Alex McCormick (deceased) Ballycastle
56. Dickie Duffin and Pat McBride
57. Paddy Stewart, Drumawillan
58. McCahan scrapbook
59. Andy McKinley
60. McCahan scrapbook
61. McCahan, Chapter B. p11
62. McCahan, Chapter B. p16
63. Pat McBride, Ballyreagh
64. "Oh, Maybe it Was Yesterday", plate 52. Glens of Antrim
     Historical Society,1980
65. McCahan, Chapter B. p16
66. Undated cutting
67. Jimmy McVeigh, Arcavally
68. John Holbrook, Ballycastle
69. Undated cutting from the Irish Weekly, Belfast
70. Jamie Davidson
71. Mick McAuley, Ballyvoy
72. Jamie Davidson
73. Griffith pp 67-75, 1829
74. Raymond McBride

75. Jamie Davidson
76. Lent Assizes, 1815 p26
77. Jamie Davidson
78. Griffith's Valuation, p52
79. Griffith's Valuation, p47
80. Spring Assizes 1899, p103
81. John Duncan, Drumnakeel
82. Jamie Davidson
83. Anna Edwards, Coolnagoppagh
84. Place-names of Northern Ireland, p171
85. Henry Joe McHenry (deceased)
86. Jim Sunstrum, Canmore Alberta, Canada
87. Paddy McBride (deceased) Carey Mill, and formerly of Greenans, Glenshesk
88. Jamie Davidson
89. Joe Lyden
90. Jamie Davidson
91. Andy McKinley
92. Dickie Duffin
93. Seamus Clarke and Dickie Duffin
94. Chronicle, 3/10/1990
95. Owen Quinn, Dublin
96. Grand Jury Presentation Book for County Antrim, 1814 Summer Assizes, p28
97. Bun-na-Margie, p44. Francis Joseph Bigger M.R.I.A. F.R.S.A. Belfast, 1898
98. Glynns Vol 21, p72; Glynns Vol 23, pp 55,56,57,59
99. Tessie McMichael, (deceased) Straid
100. Charlie Neill (deceased) Novally
101. Rosemary McCaughan, Ballycastle
102. By the Moyle Shore, Vol.1, p132 and Glynns Vol.10 p47
103. Dickie Duffin
104. Pat McBride, Ballyreagh
105. Jamie Davidson
106. Seamus Clarke
107. Blossoms from the Hedgerows, pp 75-76. W&G Baird Ltd, Belfast
108. Seamus Clarke
109. Sean Jennings (deceased)
110. Seamus Clarke
111. By the Moyle Shore, Vol.2 p.48
112. Seamus Clarke

113. Jamie Davidson
114. Dickie Duffin
115. Glynns Vol.21, pp 70,71,75,76
116. Heads and Hearths; the hearth money rolls and poll tax returns for Co. Antrim 1660 – 69, p119. S.T. Carleton, Belfast, 1991.
117. Dickie Duffin
118. Glynns Vol 1 pp 12,14
119. Slater's Directory of Ireland
120 Coleraine Chronicle, 24/4/1858
121 Glynns Vol 5, p 56
122. Ballycastle Union, p 45
123. Coleraine Chronicle, 25/5/1991

Maritime and Place names Miscellany.

Bakewells Field; Torr, formerly held by the Bakewell family, now of Ballycastle.[1]

Bible, The; a square rock off Fair Head where seals basked.[2]

Butlers Port; Gobb[3]

Campbells Rock; Torr, named after Jamie Campbell, - brother in law of Dickie Duffin.[4]

Casnatinny; at Freestone Point

Cursing on board a boat was frowned on in the past, even when one had suffered an injury.[5]

Cuckoo storms; the storms often coincided with the arrival of the cuckoo.[6]

Diamond, The; Ballyvoy at the crosroads.[7]

Donal Gorm; this was a Rathlin term for the sea.[8]

Fanny Kerdy's Field; near Culfeightrin Rectory; This field was owned by a woman who had a pub at the Quay.[9]

Flood Rock; off Fair Head.[10]

Fluke Bed; off The Pans Rocks.[11] The flat fish were once plentiful and were fished at Parkend, and Boheeshane, Ballintoy. They were bought by Morton, Ballycastle and Sawyers, Belfast.[12]

Garden of Carey; Carey Mill.[13]

Gasparo; a fish about twice the size of a herring, which were caught at Duncan's Bay and the Bull Point, Rathlin.[14]

Ghostyin; snare used to trap sea-birds on Rathlin.[15]

The Horseshoe; a large bend on the Carey River at Drumahitt, sometimes called Caldwells Horseshoe.[16]

The Horse Rodden; at the Waterfall, Carrickmore.[17]

The Inlet; the road between the former Glenshesk School and the main road.[18]

John Henry's Steps; a spot where the Glen River narrows between large rocks, and one can cross over. It is close to the Big Bridge. The John Henry, who is commemorated here, has now been forgotten.[19]

Keel Brae; at the Church ruins, Drumeeny.[20]

Lacknatraw; at the base of Fair Head.[21]

Lateen; another name for a drontheim, the traditional fishing boat used on the North Coast.[22]

Legahapple; a hollow East of Benvan House.[23]

Louby; a rock at the Gobb, the name is never used now.[24]

Lookout Rock; Benvan.[25]

The Leap; waterfall at Carrickmore.[26]

Malavore; (the big hill brow) above Corrymeela.[27]

Malawee; (yellow hill brow) above Carrickmore.[28]

May Bulk; also referred to as the May Fleece, was the name given to the seaweed which was washed ashore with the Cockcoo storms in the month of May. This seaweed was collected by farmers for use as fertilizer on their potatoe crops and also on turnips.[29]

Mearn; a small headed fish usually caught inshore, but also in deep water. Mearn were full of scales and were used in soups.[30]

Moonbows; this is the term given to rainbows when they occur at night, they have been witnessed by the late Sammy Wilkinson on a few occasions.[31]

Nancy's Rock; a rock between the Iron Stage and Gobb.[32]

Paddy's Field; a field at Benvan named after a Paddy Bán Scally.[33]

Pinnacle; a dangerous fishing location at Carrickmore.[34]

Pict's Cave, Fair Head; is referred to in 19th century accounts of the area, but today its location is unknown.

Pigeon Cave/Cove; below Benvan.[35]

Purgatory, Torr; this is a good location to fish lythe but access is difficult and one has to descend down a rope.[36]

Raghery; The old name for Rathlin but it is seldom heard today.

Rathlinman's Champ; a meal consisting of mashed potatoes with raisins. This was popular in many Ballycastle working class families during the 1930's – 1940's.[37]

Rat's Tail; This was used as bait by at least one local fisherman.[38]

Red Brae; Benvan; so named from the red soil here.[39]

Rosie's Hill; This is a field named along the lane to the gravel quarry at Drumnakeel.[40]

Salmon; the fish often leap out of the water, sometimes landing tail first. This occurs when the salmon are attempting to shake off lice.[41]

Sandy Nose; Point near Marconi's Cottage.[42]

Scad; also called horse mackerel, they are a fish of Southern waters and are about twice the size of herring.[43]

Sea of Moyle; generally considered to stretch from Malin Head, Inishowen to Islay and and southwards to Larne and eastwards to Loch Ryan.

Seals; were once shot and skinned in the Ballycastle area. The pelts were then sold to a Belfast firm.[44]

Shallop; One of a number of names for the traditional North coast boat.[45]

The Skerriaghs/Skurriagh; rocks at Gobb.[46]

Slaters; were used as bait to fish for cuddins at Carrickmore.[47]

Sronbane; west of Carrickmore.

St Patrick's Tower; a rip tide off Torr, which rises in an abrupt sheet of water.[48]

Taymouth Castle Bay; takes its name from the vessel known as the "Cut and Run" which was lost near Torr, in early January 1867.[49]

Thunder; fish will not take bait while there is thunder in the air.[50]

Top Boot; A field name in Ballynagard.[51]

Whirly Hills; Craigfad.[52]

References

1. Jim Bakewell (deceased), Ballycastle
2. Denis Boyd (deceased), Ballycastle
3. John McAuley, Manchester
4. Dickie Duffin
5. Sammy Wilkinson
6. Jack Coyles
7. Jamie Davidson
8. Alex Morrison
9. Jamie Davidson
10. Dickie Duffin
11. Dickie Duffin
12. Sammy Wilkinson
13. Jamie Davidson
14. Sammy Wilkinson and Sonny Norton, Ballycastle
15. Alex Morrison
16. Dickie Duffin
17. John Hill, Ballycastle
18. Joe Lyden (deceased) Glenshesk
19. Billy Boylan
20. John McCarry, Portrush formerly Glenshesk
21. Ordinance Survey Maps
22. Sammy Wilkinson
23. Chrissie Laverty, Ballycastle, formerly Murlough
24. Jamie McKiernan (deceased) Ballycastle
25. Chrissie Laverty
26. Jamie Davidson
27. Pat McBride (deceased) Ballyreagh
28. Pat McBride (deceased) Ballyreagh
29. Dickie Duffin and Jamie Davidson
30. Sammy Wilkinson
31. Sammy Wilkinson
32. Jamie Davidson
33. Chrissie Laverty
34. Dickie Duffin
35. Dickie Duffin

36. Dickie Duffin
37. Johnny Parker, Birmingham, formerly Ballycastle
38. Johnny Parker, Birmingham, formerly Ballycastle
39. Chrissie Laverty
40. Jamie Davidson
41. Jack Coyles
42. John Hill
43. Sammy Wilkinson and Sonny Norton
44. Dickie Duffin
45. Sonny Norton, Sammy Wilkinson and others
46. John Hill
47. Dickie Duffin
48. Dickie Duffin
49. Glynns Vol 14 pp 12 –15
50. Dickie Duffin
51. Jamie Davidson
52. John McClements

Index

162

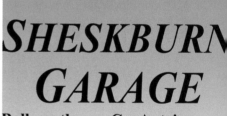